Machine Dressmaking

Machine Dressmaking

Brenda Redmile

B.T. Batsford Ltd, London

Filmset by Latimer Trend & Company Ltd, Plymouth
and printed in Great Britain by
The Anchor Press Ltd
Tiptree, Essex
for the publishers
B. T. Batsford Ltd
4 Fitzhardinge Street
London W1H 0AH

Contents

Acknowledgments

My grateful thanks are extended to: Ray Neale of Elna Sewing Machines (GB) Ltd. for his assistance in obtaining many of the photographs used in this publication; Anne Kerr of Tootal Sewing Products for providing me with photographs and information on dressmaking aids supplied by the company; Caroline Spawton and my daughters Wendy, Alison and Susan who wear the various garments featured throughout the book.

Introduction

A sewing machine forms part of the furniture and effects of a large number of homes. The type of machine may vary from an old treadle or hand machine, often handed down from mother to daughter to granddaughter, or it may be a swing needle of the very latest in technology – a fully electronically programmed machine. Despite the fact that so many people own sewing machines, many do not use them fully or to their best advantage. Often people are dissatisfied with the first garment they make, usually saying 'it looks home made', so they never attempt a second. There the machine remains, stored away in the corner of a room, probably only surfacing to run up the occasional pair of curtains for the spare room.

Having been a designer for the clothing trade for over 20 years I have seen many changes in making-up techniques. Of course industrial sewing machines have advanced too but the basic domestic zig zag machine is capable of achieving almost the same results as the lockstitch and overlock machines used in factories. Whichever kind of machine you own or indeed are thinking of purchasing, a sound knowledge of the skills involved in dressmaking will greatly add to your enjoyment of using the sewing machine. When disappointed dressmakers show me their efforts, I usually find the 'home made' look is a result of old-fashioned methods such as bulky seams, double turned hems, bulky facings and the like. What saddens me most is, when I enquire as to the kind of sewing machine they own, the dressmaker often has a fairly modern one or at least a basic zig zag machine, but is still making clothes by using methods popular at the turn of the century!

There are no hard and fast rules involved in making clothes and in many cases there are several ways of achieving the same finished result. Also the same or very similar technique may be used for dealing with different parts of the garment. For example, a waist band may be made and stitched onto a skirt in the same way as a cuff is stitched to a sleeve; the technique used for a placket in a sleeve, skirt or bodice is basically the same procedure regardless of position. Once these and other similarities are recognised the home dressmaker will be able to make up garments much more quickly and confidently.

Familiarizing oneself with various pattern pieces is extremely useful and saves a great deal of time at the cutting and making up stages. For this reason I have shown the relevant pattern shapes alongside the particular technique being described. It is of course valuable to have knowledge of pattern making to aid your understanding of dressmaking. The instructions for cutting all the pattern pieces used in this book are given in *Make Your Own Dress Patterns*, B. T. Batsford, 1980, for those who wish to carry out the complete operation of garment making. One great advantage of cutting the pattern for yourself from your own measurements is that you know it will fit and so tacking becomes unnecessary. I know many find fitting a garment frustrating, but I do feel people tend to place too much emphasis on this particular task. Commercial patterns in general are cut on the generous side and it is as well to make a check measurement and adjustment where necessary before cutting. All the techniques used within this book are generally standard and would be those a dressmaker would normally encounter when working from a commercial pattern.

My aim is to take the tedium out of making up. Clothes made in factories are cut and made up quickly and with today's easy styles there is no reason why the home dressmaker should labour for unnecessary hours over basic tasks. Fabric textures vary considerably and therefore a fair amount of thought must be given in selecting the best method and most suitable machine stitch for the job. Don't be afraid to try a different method if you think it is easier or more suited to your ability. Take note of how garments are made when they are hanging on rails in stores. You will be surprised at the simple making up methods adopted for various features on clothing, but they often carry a not so simple price tag!

Abbreviations
RS – right side of fabric
WS – wrong side of fabric

1 Machine variables

Instructions on how to thread your machine are given in the manufacturer's booklet together with details of how to obtain a perfect sewing stitch by adjusting tension settings. There are many people who are almost afraid of touching the tension controls because they fear the consequences. Indeed many students and keen amateur dressmakers have confessed to me that they have found it necessary to take the machine into a machine repair expert after altering the tensions because they were unable to obtain a satisfactory stitch again.

I would agree with the school of thought that once your machine is set up and the tension is satisfactory, leave well alone. However, a machine owner should be familiar with the variables of the machine, such as upper and lower tension, stitch length, presser foot pressure and the forward and reverse movement of the machine. It is interesting and worthwhile to switch on your machine and operate the foot control without threading the machine or feeding fabric under the presser foot. Observe the way in which the feed teeth operate for forward and reverse movement but be sure to have the presser foot in the raised position. It is unwise to run the machine with the presser foot against the teeth.

Upper tension

To test the tension try a row of stitching on scraps of fabric, preferably woven fabric, in the first instance. If you have a piece of cotton gingham or striped cotton print this is excellent to work on. You can use the print as a guide to sewing a straight line. Wind a spool with a general purpose thread suitable for use with cotton. Sylko supreme is a cotton covered polyester thread which I find suitable for most fabrics. Thread the machine with the same quality thread but preferably a different colour. Be sure to use threads of the same make on both the spool and upper part of the machine. Cut two strips of cloth approximately 2 in. (5 cm) wide and 12 in. (30 cm) long. Set stitch width at straight stitch and the length at about the midway point on your dial or stitch length lever. Most machines have stitch length markings 1 to 4 and for this test select a position between 2 and 3. Now set your upper tension dial. Seek advice from your machine manual here. In general most makes of domestic sewing machines have the upper tension dials numbered 1 to 9 and advise a setting of around 4 for general purpose use. To increase the upper tension turn the dial to higher numbers between 4 and 9 and to reduce the tension, turn to numbers lower than 4. To draw up the lower thread hold the end of the thread from the needle in your left hand and with your right hand turn the drive wheel towards you, thus lowering the needle into the throat plate. Continue turning the wheel and holding the needle thread until the needle rises and brings up the spool thread in a loop. Free the loop by hand and place both needle and spool threads under the presser foot ready to start sewing. Check that the spool is turning in the correct direction as detailed in your machine manual. Turn the drive wheel by hand to ensure that the needle is in the highest position. Place the two strips of fabric together over the feed plate having previously pinned these to hold them together. Position the fabric so that one end is under the raised presser foot and now lower the presser foot. Lower the needle into the cloth by turning the wheel by hand. Never start sewing with the foot control until you have lowered the needle into the fabric first, by hand turning the drive wheel. Now sew three stitches forward and then three in reverse, change back to forward and machine a straight row of stitching to the end of the strip, finishing with three or four back stitches. The reverse stitching is controlled either by the stitch length lever or by a reverse button depending on the make of machine.

To remove the fabric from the machine make sure the needle is in its uppermost position, lift the presser foot and pull the threads to the rear keeping the top thread between the presser foot groove. Cut the thread with the cutter provided on the machine. If the threads will not allow you to pull the fabric easily this is because the needle and take up lever are not in the highest position. Adjust the position by turning the drive wheel by your right hand and you will feel the tension ease on the threads being pulled by your left hand.

1

If all the variable machine settings are correct you will have before you a perfect seam stitch with the upper thread interlocking with the lower thread in between the two layers of cloth as in *figure 1*. The two layers of fabric should start and finish together and the stitches should measure about 14 to the inch (5 cm). However, if this is not the case alterations to the settings must be made. To correct the faults first examine the stitches carefully. Note the colours to identify where the fault lies. If the bottom coloured thread shows in loops along the top of the fabric the tension is too tight. In effect the thread is being stretched so tight that the lower colour is pulled to the surface (*figure 2*).

2

In this case reduce the tension by turning to a lower setting. If the top colour thread shows through to the bottom of the two layers of cloth the tension is too loose and this time the loose thread is being pulled through by the lower thread (*figure 3*). Increase the tension to remedy this by turning to a higher setting. After adjusting the tension try the line of machining again until you are completely satisfied and you are able to see only one colour on the top of the fabric and the other colour underneath.

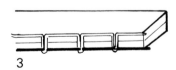

3

10

Spool tension

A perfect stitch should be achieved by adjustment of the upper tension. The spool tension is usually set for the machine and it should not normally be necessary to make any adjustment here. However, if you have not been successful in obtaining a perfect stitch by means of the upper tension adjustment you may find that the trouble stems from the spool tension. When your spool is placed in the spool case the thread passes through a slot and is drawn under the tension spring. The tension spring is regulated by adjusting the screw by means of a small screw driver (*figure 4*). To increase the tension turn the screw clockwise and to reduce the tension turn in an anti-clockwise direction. This may well be the cause of the trouble and is worthy of consideration when other methods fail. If the tension is too loose it will cause the lower thread to be pulled through to the top layer in a similar way to that illustrated in *figure 2*, or if it is too tight it may pull the upper thread down to the lower surface as in *figure 3*.

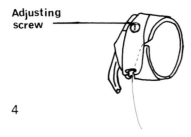

Adjusting screw

4

Should it be necessary to adjust the spool tension I would advise that you start again with the upper thread tension set at number 4. This way you will be able to determine which tension is in need of adjustment. If your machine is the type that has a built-in spool case, the adjustment screw is the one situated to the side of the tension spring. It is not uncommon to experience difficulty with stitching, owing to a loose spool tension, after one has been using thick threads or shearing elastic on the spool. The thicker threads can force the spring apart unnaturally and adjustment is required before general purpose thread can again be used satisfactorily. When using shearing elastic the screw is adjusted as a matter of course to control the amount of stretch. This is dealt with in more detail in chapter 4.

If you find that your test sample puckers this may be caused by the incorrect setting of one of the tensions already discussed, but it is possible that the stitch length is at fault. Shorten the stitch and try again. The length of stitch will require altering for different thicknesses of cloth.

When you are satisfied with the machine stitching on your strips of cotton fabric, experiment with other textures. The machine will probably need slight adjustments for different types of cloth. Varying textures may also make it necessary to adjust the pressure on the presser foot. Sometimes the top layer of fabric will move, causing ripples. When this happens there is too much pressure from the presser foot. Release the tension on the presser foot slightly and try again. If the fabric does not feed smoothly the pressure on the presser foot may be too light and should be increased accordingly. Newer machines have automatic pressure controls which ensure that the correct pressure is used for all fabrics.

Needles

The machine needles used also play an important part in obtaining a perfect stitch. It is best to keep a selection pack of general purpose needles of various sizes with your machine. These are suitable for use with most woven fabrics and some, but not all, knitted fabrics. Difficulty is often experienced when machining knitted fabric and blame is all too often thrown onto the machine or the fabric when the real reason is the machine needle. Because of the structure of certain knitted fabrics, general purpose needles often fail to penetrate the material. The needle pushes against the fabric and instead of passing through the two thicknesses of fabric and interlocking with the lower thread, it depresses the material into the feed plate and springs back again without making the correct stitch. The result is a very 'hit and miss' line of stitching or no stitches at all. Ball point needles are specially made to overcome the problems experienced when machining knitted fabrics and these are sold in a selection of sizes. A considerable amount of thought has been given to the manufacture of machine needles and apart from the general purpose and ball point needles mentioned special needles are now available for stretch fabric, as well as needles for sewing leather, oilskin and suede.

So, if you are not happy with the result of your machine stitching the needle you are using must certainly be considered as a possible cause for the poor work produced. You are strongly advised to try alternative needles before criticizing the fabric or the machine.

When you change a needle be sure to have the needle fitted into the machine securely and in the correct way. All machine needles have a flat side and a rounded side at the top of the needle. Following down from the round side of the needle you will find a groove down the centre of the main staff of the needle. This groove must always be on the side from which the machine is threaded. Therefore, if the machine is threaded from front to back the needle groove should face you and the flat side top of the needle will be towards the back. If the needle is threaded from the left the groove should face the left and the flat side should be on the right.

Stitch length and width

Having adjusted your machine to produce a perfect straight stitch now try a basic zig zag stitch. Ensure that your machine has the correct presser foot fitted for zig zag stitching. The zig zag foot has a wide slot for the needle to pass through rather than a single hole. All zig zag machines have a stitch width control which determines the amount of swing of the needle from left to right. A zig zag machine is sometimes referred to as a swing needle machine.

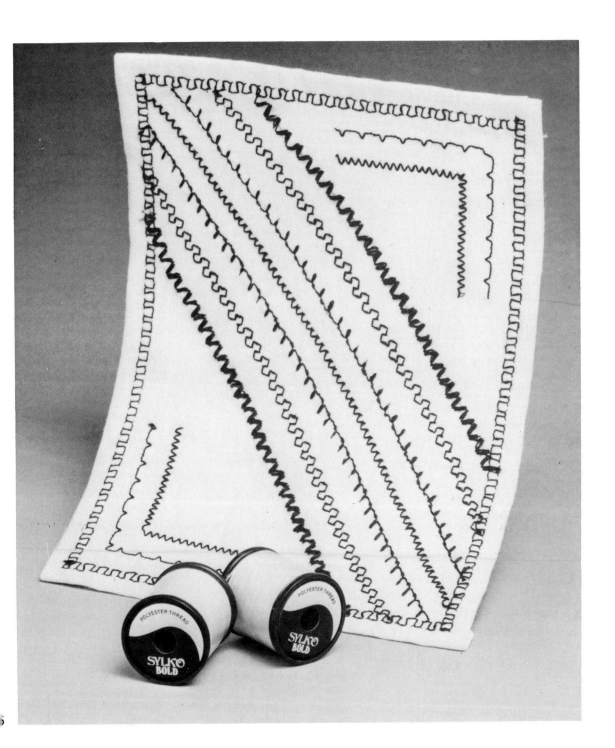

The maximum swing is generally not more than $\frac{3}{16}$ in. (5 mm). The width control is usually a lever which may be set adjacent to the appropriate width of zig zag. This is marked either by a number or a zig zag symbol. The numbers are usually marked 0 to 4 – 0 being straight stitch and 4 being the widest zig zag. Some machines have a numbered or symbolled dial for setting the stitch width.

To acquaint yourself with the versatility of the zig zag stitch, try the following exercise. Set the stitch width at 2 (medium zig zag) and the stitch length at between 2 and 3 (medium length). Sew a few stitches and then open up the width of the zig zag by gradually moving the stitch width to 3 and 4. Now shorten the length of the stitch to between 0 and 1 and practise satin stitch reducing and widening the stitch width gradually to observe the effect. Adjust the stitch length to gain experience in gauging the correct spacing for various finishes.

The tension settings may need to be altered for zig zag stitching, and here the same principles apply as described for straight stitching. When the spool thread shows on the top of the stitching the upper tension is too tight and if the upper thread is pulled through to the underneath the tension is too loose. Make the necessary adjustments.

Programme selection

The stitch length and width are the main variables of the basic swing needle machine. Most basic machines also have a facility for moving the needle position from centre to left or right. This facility can be very useful for certain operations such as button-holing and hemming.

Semi-automatic machines have several general purpose stitches built in. These usually include a basic zig zag stitch, a blind hem stitch, a scallop edge stitch, and an elastic stitch. The required stitch is selected by a dial or lever which once set into position programmes the machine to work the chosen stitch. The width and length of the stitches are controlled by operating the appropriate lever or dial.

Automatic machines have a much wider selection of patterns. These machines often have drop-in cams each marked with the various patterns and when the cam is in position and the appropriate controls are set quite attractive stitches are made. The machine will stitch a programmed shape automatically moving the needle from left to right and the feed plate will operate in forward and reverse movement. All the machinist has to do is guide the fabric as for straight stitching. There are dozens of different patterns available, some provided with the machine when purchased and others offered as extras. Some decorative stitches can be very useful for the home dressmaker and examples of the use of some of these stitches are given in other chapters.

Practise the various programme refinements of your machine and try using different threads for greater effect (*figure 5*). You will find it useful as you progress with dressmaking to know exactly what your machine will do.

14

2 Cutting and assembling a garment

The preparation and cutting of fabric is extremely important and short cuts must not be taken here. In a factory where clothes are cut for mass production the cloth is laid up directly from the roll. Many layers are cut at one time but great care is taken to ensure the cloth is lying straight. At home your piece of fabric for one garment will have been folded in a bag and carried from the retailer and will probably have numerous creases in it. Press the fabric carefully on the wrong side, setting the iron thermostat according to the constituent fibres of your fabric. Use your general domestic iron and smooth out the fabric singly, pressing away the fold. The right side is usually folded inside and it is a good idea to mark the wrong side with a X in tailors' chalk. Although commercial patterns advise in their lay instructions to place certain pattern pieces to the fold, it is still a good practice to iron out the original 'hard pressed' fold at this early stage. Fold it more lightly for cutting purposes at a later time. If you usually use a steam iron you will find that steam is probably needed to flatten the fold. When using a dry iron it will be necessary to use a slightly damp cloth over the fold. Most cloths are preshrunk but you may find that if it is necessary to use a damp cloth or steam on the fold of a wool cloth it may shrink a little more. In this case you should press the whole piece of cloth singly with a damp cloth or steam iron. This helps to avoid any further shrinkage when pressing seams during making up. Allow the steam to evaporate before moving onto the next part of the cloth.

After pressing the cloth try to handle it as little as possible for a while. Try to lay it flat on a table or over the ironing board for an hour to allow the cloth to air completely. Never use a damp cloth on a fabric before testing a small area to ensure that it does not water mark.

While pressing, examine your fabric carefully for any marks or flaws and mark these with a pin. This enables the flaw to be easily noticed when placing the pattern in position.

When you use a new commercial pattern you will find it necessary to cut away the surplus paper around each pattern piece. Some pattern companies suggest cutting through the paper and cloth simultaneously but I value my cloth cutting scissors too much for this. I would not recommend anyone to cut paper and cloth with the same scissors. A general purpose pair of scissors may be used for cutting paper but for cutting cloth a flat sided sharp pair of scissors is as essential to the home dressmaker as her sewing machine. Take great care of your fabric scissors, be careful not to drop them to damage the blades and guard them jealously from the rest of the family. Scissors are personal pieces of equipment and rather like a fountain pen should only be used by their owners.

Having prepared the fabric and pattern you are now ready to cut the garment. Allow yourself plenty of room to lay the fabric out as suggested on the laying up sheet if you are using a commercial pattern. If you are using your own make of pattern, ensure that you can fit all the pattern pieces on clearly. Finding a large enough surface does present problems to many home dressmakers. The kitchen work surface is probably the best choice in the home, but since most surfaces are not more than 24 in. (60 cm) wide and some less than that it does have great limitations. The kitchen surface does have the advantage of being hard and smooth and is usually resistant to scratches from scissors, pins etc. The dining table is usually wider but the polished surface would not stand up to scissors and pins scratching against it and should be covered first with thick card. There are, on the market, some cutting boards marked out in square centimetres intended to lie over the table for cutting purposes. These boards measure 180 cm × 106 cm approx. and fold away to 30 cm × 106 cm when not in use. I would strongly recommend using one of these boards if you only have a choice of the polished surface of a dining table or a carpeted floor to cut out on.

In most cases your pattern instructions will give a laying up diagram showing a folded piece of cloth with the selvedges together. It is worth mentioning here that it is not a good policy to use the selvedge as part of the garment because the yarns used may be liable to shrinkage. Fold your fabric with the right sides inside if possible to keep it clean and make subsequent marking easier. Press your fingers along the fold position and smooth the fabric across the selvedge. Put an occasional pin about 1 in. (2·5 cm) in from the fold to hold this straight and pin the selvedge together at regular intervals. Remember that the length of cloth may not have been cut exactly straight at the retailers and that you must get the fold correct and the selvedges matching. The selvedge and fold are the straight grain of the fabric.

Observe whether there is a pattern on your fabric with a one-way design or nap. Textured threads are brushed in one direction down the cloth. In these instances each pattern piece must be positioned on the cloth the same way up i.e. growing flowers must grow upwards and long pile fabrics should fall or be brush downwards. Where the pattern is reversible it is possible to dovetail the pattern pieces to use a little less fabric. Be careful not to be caught out when reversing pattern pieces or dovetailing. Sometimes it is possible for what appears to be a plain fabric to shine a slightly different shade when turned the other way round. Jersey knit fabrics are particularly prone to this shading difference and I prefer to try and keep all my pattern pieces running the same way for the whole garment.

Matching patterns such as checks and stripes needs extra care and planning. It is best to open the fabric out singly and draw around each pattern piece with tailors' chalk before cutting. Remember to turn the pattern piece over for the second copy to ensure that you cut a pair. This way you can see the pattern more clearly and be sure that the corresponding notch marks fall on the same position of the fabrics pattern. In many cases the notches are numbered in pairs to enable the home dressmaker to know at a glance which seams join each other in make up.

Whether the cloth is patterned or plain always place the largest pattern pieces onto the cloth first and then fill in with the smaller pattern pieces.

Pay particular attention to the markings on the pattern pieces and acquaint yourself with their meanings. Pattern markings are well standardized now and one soon becomes familiar with the symbols used. Nowadays most patterns are printed and the instructions are therefore marked adjacent to the various symbols used. Check that the grain lines on your pattern lie parallel with the selvedge or fold of your fabric. Measure from the selvedge of your fabric to the arrow at each end of the line marked on the pattern to ascertain that the grain is exactly straight. This is important because most clothes are cut with the straight grain, the warp threads, running from shoulder to hem and if this is not exactly straight the garment will not hang correctly. Notice which pieces must be placed to a fold and place the edge of the pattern paper right up to the fold. The pattern pieces most usually placed to the fold are the centre back or centre front. If you do not place these exactly on the fold you will undoubtedly cut a garment that is too big.

When you have fitted all the pattern pieces onto the fabric, pin these securely through both thicknesses of fabric. Be sure to keep the pattern and both layers of cloth lying flat. Make sure you have all the necessary pattern pieces required for the style you are to make. Start to cut the largest pieces first. Cut with even clear cuts holding your scissors with the flat edge running along the work surface. Cut close to the edge of your pattern pieces, cutting through the double layer of fabric. As each piece is cut place it to one side with the pattern piece still pinned into position for subsequent marking.

I prefer to use dressmakers' tracing paper and a tracing wheel for markings. To use this place the waxed tracing paper between the pattern and the wrong side of the fabric. The coloured waxed side of the tracing paper should be next to the fabric. Full instructions are given on the tracing paper packet. Use the tracing wheel to mark such details as darts, button and buttonhole positions, pleats, notches and pocket positions. It is not necessary to mark all the seam construction lines.

There are other aids on the market for transferring pattern markings onto cloth and it is a good idea to try some of these to find the one most suited to your needs.

When all the necessary pattern markings are transferred to the wrong side of the fabric take out the pins and remove the pattern. You are now ready to start sewing but handle the fabric as little as possible. Take great care not to stretch any areas cut on the bias e.g. armhole and neck curves. Where required, iron a suitable weight of interlining onto the wrong side of the fabric.

You may like to assemble the garment temporarily to check the fit. To do this, pin the seams, matching the notches and machine tack these remembering to leave the necessary opening to enable you to fit the garment.

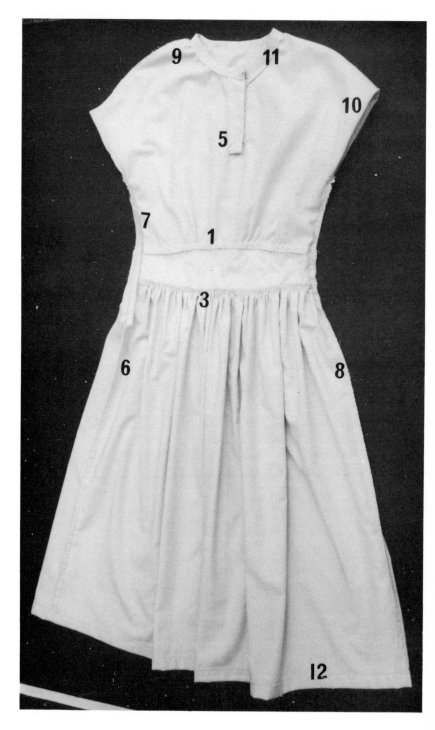

6

You may be able to make a satisfactory test fitting by only pinning the garment along the seams. Garments manufactured in factories are of course not fitted to individuals but are cut to stock sizes. It is a great advantage to be able to make your own patterns from a basic block made to your measurements. This saves considerable time and frustration over fitting. You can be sure that the garment will fit across the shoulders, cross back and around the bust, hip and armhole when you use your own patterns. These are the areas that frequently need attention when commercial patterns are used. When you fit the garment, whether pinned or machine tacked, try it on with the wrong side to the outside. This way it is easier to make any necessary adjustments. Pin where alterations are needed and then mark any deviation from the normal seam allowance with tailors' chalk.

Before all the seams may be machined and finished, design features such as pleats, pockets and collars must be dealt with. The techniques used in making these features are given in the appropriate chapters.

There are no hard and fast rules concerning the order in which the seams are sewn in any particular garment as so much depends on the position of seams. However, having said that, I would advise that a dressmaker tries to get into a particular method of working. Whenever possible I like to work all horizontal seams first. By horizontal I mean yokes at the chest or cross back positions and waist seams. The shoulder seams are also horizontal seams.

Figure 6 shows the inside of a dress and the numbers indicate a typical order of assembling a garment:

1 The front bodice is gathered and stitched onto the front waist panel which has been previously backed with iron-on interlining.
2 The back bodice is stitched to the back waist panel. (Not shown in photograph.)
3 The front skirt is gathered and stitched to the lower part of the waist panel.
4 The back skirt is stitched to the waist panel. (Not shown in photograph.)
5 The front placket is made. (See Chapter 8.)
6 The left side seam is joined leaving an opening for the zip fastener.
7 The zip fastener is stitched in. (See Chapter 8.)
8 The right side seam is joined.
9 The shoulder seams are joined.
10 The cap sleeve edge is hemmed and turned back. (See Chapter 7.)
11 The neck edge is finished with bias facing strip. (See Chapter 6.)
12 The skirt hem is turned and stitched.

There are of course occasions when it is necessary to stitch vertical seams first. A panel seam running from the shoulder or armhole to the waist would require stitching before the skirt could be joined to the bodice. Any darts used to create the shaping around the bust and hip positions must be stitched before other parts of the garment may be assembled.

19

3 Making-up techniques (seams and hems)

Over the last decade there have been fundamental changes in the way seams and hems are stitched. By looking at ready-made clothes hanging on the rails in shops you will be able to observe the various seam and hem finishes. Quite often dresses and blouse seams are overlocked and lockstitched together, in the same way that men's shirts have been manufactured for a long time. The raw edge of seams may be left unfinished if the fabric is of a kind that will not fray. This would have been frowned upon some time ago but now it is acceptable, as a commonsense measure, not to waste time overlocking an edge which does not require a finish. It is much better to leave the seam flat and unfinished rather than to stretch the edge by feeding it through an overlock machine which would result in a wavy edge.

With a swing needle sewing machine the home dressmaker is able to emulate the industrial techniques. The old seams, such as run and fell, French and machine turned, have become obsolete as a zig zag stitch will finish seams neatly, quickly and in the flatest possible way.

Open pressed seams

As a general rule commercial patterns allow $\frac{5}{8}$ in. (1·5 cm) seam allowances and in most cases this is acceptable. Your sewing machine will probably have marks on the needle plate graduated at $\frac{1}{8}$ in. (3 mm) intervals from the centre needle position. Since $\frac{5}{8}$ in. (15 mm) is universally accepted as a general seam allowance you may find that this position is marked with an elongated line. The lines may be marked 3, 4, 5 eighths or 10, 15, 20 mm. *Figure 7* shows the metric marking. If your machine does not have any seam markings, it is useful to mark these for yourself. To do this stick a piece of masking tape to the right of the needle and draw the lines at the correct positions measuring from the needle.

Machining a seam is therefore only a matter of lining up the raw edge of the seam along the appropriate line and then machining a straight seam. To hold the two pieces together insert pins at right angles to the stitching line. This avoids machine needle breakage. The seam edge should be on the right with the bulk of the garment on the left. Lower the needle into the seam line at approximately $\frac{3}{8}$ in. (1 cm) from the beginning. Lower the presser foot, put the machine in reverse and take about three stitches backwards almost to the end of the fabric, holding the thread ends in the left hand. It is a good idea to train

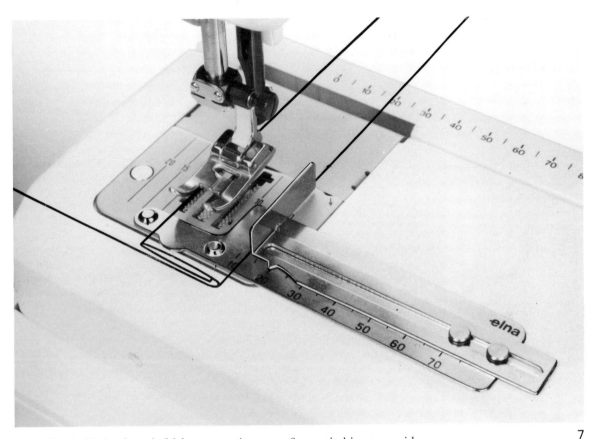

yourself to hold the threads fairly taut at the start of any stitching to avoid them snarling under the feed plate.

Now stitch forward to the end of the seam (*figure 8*). Guide the fabric as the machine is stitching by using your left hand in front, but slightly to the left of the presser foot. This should be sufficient to achieve the smooth, even feeding required. Use your right hand to keep the seam edge in line with the marking on the metal plate to the right of the presser foot. Support the bulk of the garment fabric on the table to the left of the machine. Do not allow this to hang off the table between you and the machine as this will cause dragging and result in an uneven seam.

Backstitch for four or five stitches to fasten the end of the seam. Raise the needle, by hand if necessary, lift the presser foot and draw the fabric away towards the rear of the machine without putting pressure on the needle. Keep the top thread in the presser foot groove.

There are various seam guide attachments on the market, similar to the one illustrated in *figure 7* and these are extremely useful for the beginner. Having a raised guide $\frac{3}{8}$ in. (1 cm) wide at right angles to the needle plate gives the machinist something firm to guide the raw edge against rather than

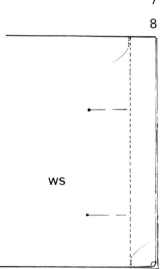

WS

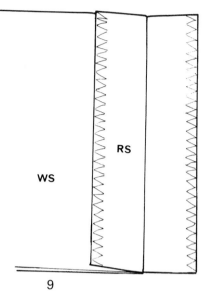

9

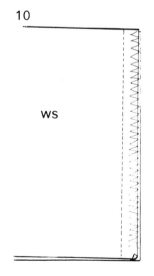

10

having to rely on the eye and skill in handling the fabric. Of course if a narrower or wider seam is required the guide may be adjusted accordingly. The quilting foot in *figure 125* may also be used as a seam guide.

This seam may now be pressed open and left unfinished if the fabric is of a type that is not likely to fray i.e. Jersey. If the edges are likely to fray you may finish these with a medium width zig zag stitch as shown in *figure 9*.

Difficulty is sometimes experienced with knitted fabrics which have a stretchy structure. The seams sometimes break open because the sewing thread does not 'give' to the same extent as the fabric. To overcome this problem stitch the main seam with the stitch length shorter than usual and the stitch width on the smallest zig zag. This will allow a little more ease in the stitching. Another suggestion to help you to overcome the difficulty is to stretch the fabric slightly as you sew the seam. This will result in a looser seam and so allow the necessary ease.

Narrow seams

When using a fine fabric for a blouse or shirt it is not essential to use an open pressed seam. Instead it is only necessary to make a $\frac{3}{8}$ in. (1 cm) or $\frac{1}{2}$ in. (1·2 cm) seam using the appropriate guide line on the metal plate. It is of course important to make the seam allowance adjustment when you are cutting the garment. Should you cut the garment with a $\frac{5}{8}$ in. (1·5 cm) seam and in fact only take up a $\frac{3}{8}$ in. (1 cm) seam the garment will make up much too large. Therefore, the $\frac{1}{4}$ in. (5 mm) must be cut off at the cutting stage.

Stitch the seam at $\frac{3}{8}$ in. (1 cm) in with the straight stitch first. Neaten the edges together with zig zag stitch as shown in *figure 10*. Although one would generally only use this method of seam with shirting fabrics it is sometimes advantageous to use when working with heavier cloths. The pleated skirt (*figure 39*) is seamed by this method taking up $\frac{1}{2}$ in. (1·2 cm) seams in this instance.

Overlocked seams

Some machines have an even more refined method of overcasting which bears greater resemblance to the industrial overlock finish (*figure 11*). This is a programmed stitch and the seam is stitched and neatened in one operation. One advantage of this finish is the amount of give afforded making its use with stretch fabrics very desirable.

Machine tacking

You may wish to use your machine to tack a seam prior to fitting. Pin the seam with pins crossing the seam line. Slacken the upper tension slightly and set the stitch length to the longest position. Machine along the sewing line using straight stitch removing the pins as you come to them. Do not use back stitches at either end of the seam. The stitches will be loose but will be strong enough to enable a fitting. The seam may gather as you stitch but this is not serious –

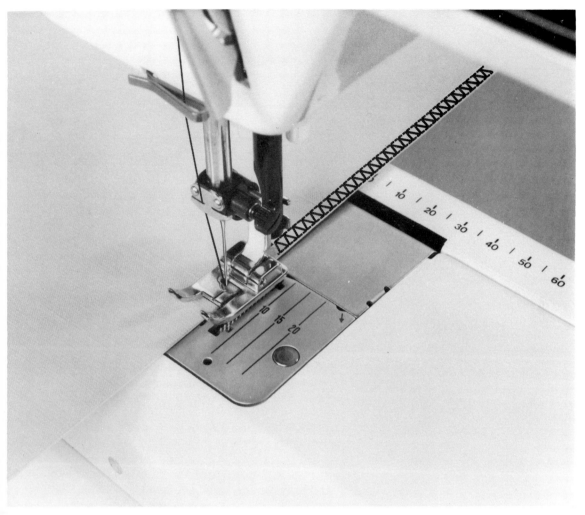

simply leave sufficient thread at the ends of your seam when you remove the garment from the machine. Smooth out the gathers by running your finger and thumb along the seam. After fitting remove the tacking by pulling the lower thread straight out.

Blind hemming

Many machines have the facility for blind hemming and this technique may be carried out in several different ways depending on the fabric being used. Generally speaking the blind stitch is a combination of narrow zig zag or straight stitches alternating with a wider zig zag at intervals of about four stitches.

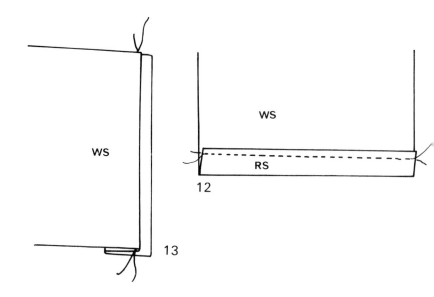

The one fold hem is used on heavy fabric. Turn the hem to the desired width and press the fold. Machine tack the hem at a position approximately $\frac{3}{8}$ in. (1 cm) from the edge (*figure 12*). Now fold the bulk of the garment to the left, over the hem turning, forming a fold along the tacking stitches and leaving the $\frac{3}{8}$ in. (1 cm) raw edge to the right (*figure 13*). Use the blind hem foot if one is supplied with your machine and set the machine at the appropriate irregular zig zag pattern. Stitch along the raw edge, neatening the edge and catching the fold at regular intervals. If your machine does not have an irregular zig zag facility you may achieve the same result by setting the zig zag at stitch width 2 for approx $\frac{1}{2}$ in. (1·2 cm) and then increasing the stitch width for one stitch in order to catch the fold. Continue this procedure until the hem is completed. Now remove the garment from the machine and pull out the machine tacking. Allow the hem to fall into position. The very tiny stitches catching the hem will sink into the garment fabric and the resulting hem will be almost invisible.

As you become more experienced at blind hemming you will find it unnecessary to machine tack in the first instance. The guide used in *figure 14* is ideal for working without previously tacking because the fold is lying between the foot and the guide.

The two fold hem is a similar blind hem but with the raw edge neatened by a very small turning. Turn the hem to the required width having first turned in the raw edge. Machine tack if desired as before. Stitch the hem using the stitch which gives a straight stitch and occasional zig zag. When stitching make sure the zig zag stitches catch just inside the fold and the straight stitches secure the turned-in raw edge (*figure 15*). If you do not have a facility on your machine for irregular stitching you may operate the dials by hand. Work about five

24

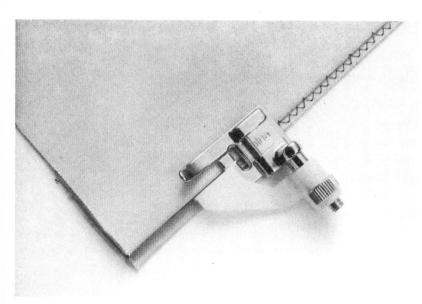

14

15

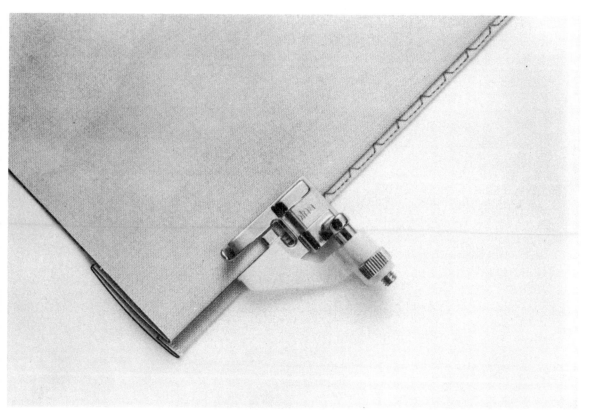

16

stitches straight then zig zag for one stitch using a medium width stitch to catch the fold. Continue in this way to complete the hem. This method is obviously not as quick as that of the automatic machine. I do recommend the blind hem facility to dressmakers buying new machines. The finished result will be a nice flat hem which is a great improvement on the old herring bone stitched hem with the inevitable unsightly ridge showing on the right side of the garment.

Narrow hem

Another way to finish the hem is to use the narrow hem turner foot. This method is particularly useful where a frill is to be hemmed. The hemmer foot guides the fabric through a scroll turning the raw edge in and making a finished hem about $\frac{1}{4}$ in. (5 mm) wide. The main difficulty encountered by beginners is in feeding the fabric into the scroll to commence the hem. It is best to raise the hemmer foot and feed the fabric into the scroll of the hemmer with the right hand. Ease the first part of the hem under the needle position before lowering the hemmer foot into the sewing position. Hold the edge of the fabric between the thumb and forefinger of your right hand and feed only enough material into the hemmer to fill out the scroll. Ease the bulk of the garment along with the left hand as the hem is stitched to assist in even feeding. The hem may be stitched using straight stitch or zig zag as shown in *figure 16*. This is a very quick method of hemming and I would recommend its wider use as it is especially useful with fine fabrics. The frills and hem of the dress in *figure 17* are all finished by this method.

Top-stitched hem

Perhaps the simplest and possibly the strongest way of finishing a hem is to turn the hem to the required width and top stitch. The raw edge may be neatened with a zig zag stitch before top stitching if it is likely to fray. (Some knitted fabrics do not fray or become ravelled and so the zig zag stitching is not necessary.) This method is good for colourful, patterned fabrics as the machine stitching often blends in so well that it is almost invisible. This type of hem is used quite frequently on summer weight dresses where only a small hem is allowed. The dresses shown in *figure 126* are finished with a top stitched hem.

Scalloped or shell edging

These are also useful and decorative ways of finishing hems on fine fabrics. Basically the scallops are achieved by a zig zag stitch which in effect pulls the folded edge of the fabric tight making indentations at regular intervals. The finish is extremely valuable for finishing sleeves and frills.

To satin stitch a scallop edge, set the stitch programme for scallop stitch. The stitch width should be set at 4 and the stitch length at mid-way between 0

17

18

19

and 1 – satin stitch. Turn the hem to the width allowed and press a fold. Stitch along the fold working with the right side uppermost. Allow the small stitches to cover the edge. The needle will stitch off the fabric to the right. The wider stitches will swing to the left resulting in the scalloped effect. On the wrong side the surplus fabric may be cut away. Alternatively, if the finish is used on a sleeve the surplus hem may be left on and neatened by an elastic as shown in *figure 18*.

The shell edge is used in much the same way as the scallop edge. A combination of straight stitches with a zig zag at regular intervals (the same as blind stitch) provides the desired effect. Set the stitch width at 4 and the stitch length at 2. Machine the straight stitches about $\frac{1}{8}$ in. (3·2 mm) from the fold and allow the zig zag to be stitched off the edge of the material (*figure 19*).

4 Shaping

Darts

Darts are the most basic way of taking out fullness around the bust and hip areas. They are not always very flattering and as a designer I try to avoid their use whenever possible. Other more favoured methods of shaping are soft gathers, seam panels and pleats, all of which give a more pleasing appearance. However, if darts must be used in your garment they should be correctly machined to acquire a good finish.

Fold the cloth along the centre line of the dart with right sides together. Pin the darts in such a way that the dart markings meet. The pins should be arranged so that they cross the line for machining (*figure 20*).

To machine, place the garment under the presser foot with the widest end of the dart in line with the needle and the main piece of the garment to the left of the machine foot. Machine from the widest end to the apex of the dart removing the pins as you sew. At the apex work the last few stitches right on the fold and back stitch over these to finish off securely (*figure 21*). If a dart has an apex at each end you should start to machine a little way in from the fold and backstitch to the apex along the fold as shown in *figure 22*.

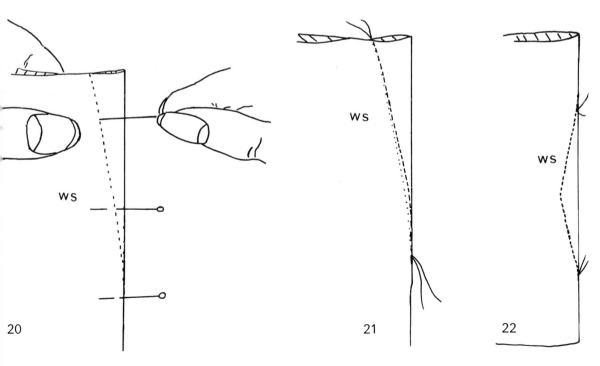

WS

20

WS

21

WS

22

Pin tucks

Pin tucking gives a refreshing alternative to darts for shaping at the front shoulder and chest area.

A twin needle and tucker foot are required to make the pin tucks. Insert the twin needle and thread each eye with matching thread. The same thread should be used on the spool. Set the stitch width to straight stitch and the stitch length to 2. The needle must be in the centre position.

Place a scrap of fabric under the tucker foot and stitch a trial tuck. The tucker foot has several grooves on the underside and the tucks are automatically formed by these (*figure 23*). It may be necessary to increase the spool tension slightly in order to hold the two top threads together underneath the work and so create a lasting tuck.

Several tucks may be made lying parallel to each other. Move the fabric slightly, placing the tuck that has just been worked into the next groove of the foot. The groove will serve as a guide and keep the tucks straight. If desired decorative stitches may be worked between groups of tucks as in *figure 68*.

23

Gathers

Gathers are used to obtain shaping and to enable one piece of a garment to fit onto another. A bodice gathered onto a yoke, a skirt gathered to a bodice or puffed sleeves gathered into the armhole are good examples.

Using one or two rows of machine stitching is the simplest way to gather the fabric. The stitching should be made in the centre of the seam allowance. Slacken the upper tension slightly and adjust the stitch length setting to the longest stitch available. This allows the lower thread to be pulled up easily. Machine one or two rows of stitching between the notches indicating where the gathers are required. At one end of the stitching wind the spool thread (the lower thread) around a pin to secure and draw up the other end of this thread until the gathers are the length required (*figure 24*). Where the gathering thread crosses a seam you may experience difficulty in pulling the thread. In this case draw the lower thread from one end first as described but only as far as the seam and then remove the anchor pin from the other end of the stitching and pull the lower thread from the other end. Pin the gathered piece on to the

24

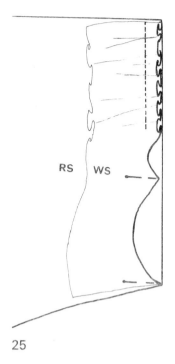

RS   WS

25

smaller piece and machine along the seam line over the gathers with the tension set for general stitching. Remove the gathering thread by pulling the lower thread.

One stage gathering is a method of obtaining a gathered effect by folding tucks into the fabric at the same time as machining a seam. The gathers made by this method are probably not as even as those made by the former method but they are also very acceptable for many purposes. The frills on the dress in *figure 17* are created by the one stage method.

First fold the longer piece (the piece to be gathered) to find half and quarter positions and mark these with pins or tailors' chalk. Take the short piece on to which the gathers are to be joined and mark the half way and quarter positions in the same way. Now pin the pieces together along the seam line with the right sides together matching half and quarter positions. If pins are used for marking remove these and leave only one at each point to join the two pieces. Where a large piece is to be gathered between pins it is advisable to pin again at a position midway between each point. The seam may now be machined with the longer piece uppermost, folding a series of small tucks as you proceed from pin to pin (*figure 25*).

This method is quick and really quite easy once you acquire the skill of judging just how much fabric should be taken up in each tuck. Avoid making all your tucks lie the same way. Fold some towards the needle and some towards you. You will find the tucks folded towards you are easier to make but slip one or two in the other direction as well. The overall finished effect will be much more pleasing (*figure 26*).

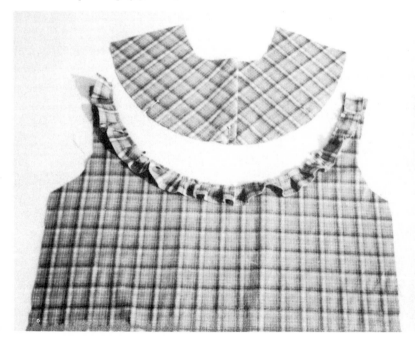

26

Elastic gathering

Another popular way of achieving gathers is to use elastic.

Three or four rows of shearing elastic worked with a contrasting thread gives a smocked effect (*figure 27*). This method is useful for skirt waists, for gathering in the waist of a shift dress or for the yoke of a blouse or dress.

Wind the spool with shirring elastic and thread the needle with either a general purpose thread or for a more pronounced appearance, a bold thread. Insert the bobbin into the case bringing the shirring elastic under the tension spring (*figure 28*). Practise machining on a spare piece of fabric before working on your garment. Cut a strip of cloth and measure its length. Work one row of stitching using a longer stitch than for general purpose sewing and measure the finished gathered piece to ascertain the amount of shaping. If the gathers are tighter than desired loosen the spool tension very slightly and practise again. It is unlikely that the spool tension will be too loose for elastic, particularly after sewing with normal sewing thread. Now practise with a second row of stitching but stretch the fabric in front of the presser foot to avoid stitching in tucks made by the previous row of gathering.

When you are satisfied with your test piece pass onto the garment. Be sure to hold both elastic and thread ends with your left hand at the start of each row of stitching. Shirring elastic does have a tendency to snarl and if it gets jammed under the foot plate it can be most frustrating.

You may experience some difficulty back stitching with an elastic thread to secure the ends. To overcome this problem machine three or four stitches at stitch length 0. This should secure the ends sufficiently until such time as they

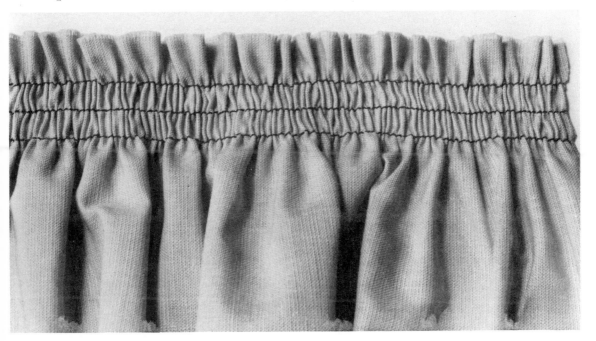

29 28

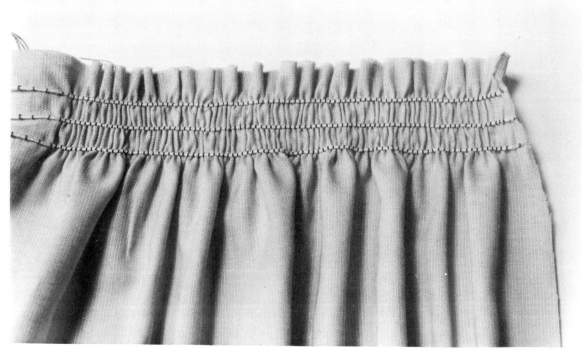

34

are caught into the seams. When seaming it is a good plan to reinforce the elasticated area with an extra row of stitching. *Figure 29* shows the shirring elastic on the wrong side of the fabric.

Remember that if you released the tension on the spool this must be re-set before you sew again with general purpose thread.

An elastic tape may be used for gathering. This may be enclosed within a hem or stretched and stitched at the same time to the wrong side of the fabric.

The elastic may be enclosed within a hem at the waist of a skirt or at the wrist of a sleeve. The waist area generally requires an elastic tape of $\frac{3}{4}$ in. (2 cm) to 1 in. (2·5 cm) wide but the wrist only needs a narrow tape of $\frac{3}{8}$ in. (1 cm) or $\frac{1}{4}$ in. (5 mm). The use of an elastic tape makes a placket unnecessary and therefore simplifies the making of a garment.

Make the hem wide enough to accommodate the elastic. Leave an opening at the seam position for the elastic to be inserted. A top stitched hem is most commonly used for this purpose. Thread the elastic through the hem keeping this flat. One end of the elastic should then be machined several times to hold it securely (*figure 30*).

Now pull up the elastic from the other end to the desired size. Pull the elastic with the right hand and hold the thumb and finger of your left hand over the hem with the elastic between to make sure that the elastic does not turn but is pulled up flat. Machine several times at the end to secure (*figure 31*). Cut off the surplus elastic and stitch the hem to complete.

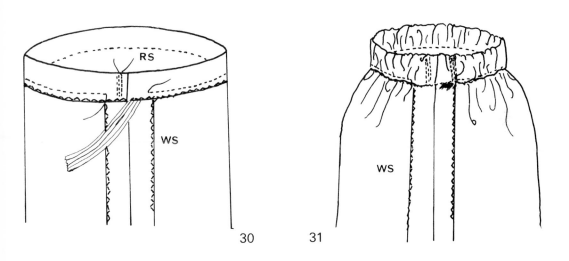

30   31

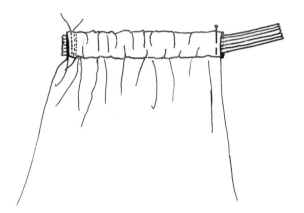

32

Alternatively you may find it easier to thread the elastic through the hem before the seam is made. In this case make the hem with the seam open. Thread the elastic through the hem keeping it flat. Machine one end to secure and pull the elastic from the other end to the desired size and pin to hold (*figure 32*). Machine the end of the elastic to secure. Remove the pin and continue with the making of the garment by machining the seams.

An elastic tape may be stretched out at the same time as zig zag stitching on the wrong side of the fabric.

Start with the elastic in the correct position on top of the wrong side of the fabric. Work a few back stitches to secure and then work forwards holding the elastic in your right hand. Use zig zag or elastic stitch at width setting 3. As you stitch stretch the elastic in front of the presser foot and the fabric will gather on to the elastic tape (*figure 33*).

33

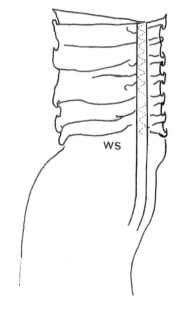

WS

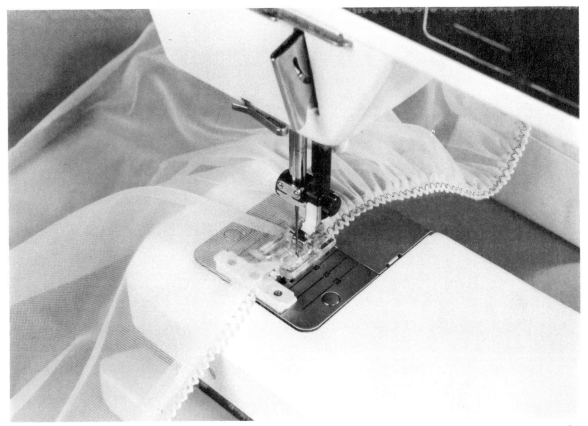

Some machines have attachments as shown in *figure 34* to fit on to the machine. This in fact stretches the elastic for you and you are able to work from the right side of the fabric with the elastic beneath.

Pleats

Pleats are generally indicated on patterns with the words 'fold line' or 'crease line'. This line is usually an unbroken line (*figure 35*). A secondary broken line indicates the position to which the pleat should be folded. Sometimes the pleat is indicated by notch marks at the top and bottom of the pleat. Whichever marking method is used the pleat position should be marked on the wrong side of the fabric. It is advisable to press in the pleats as soon as the garment has been cut and marked. Work from the right side of the fabric and place a pin at the top and bottom of the pleat fold line to transfer the marking to the right side.

Press the fold line of the pleat or pleats. Now overlap the fold line of the pleat to match the secondary markings indicating the width of the pleat (*figure 36*). Press on the wrong side this time to flatten the underpart of the

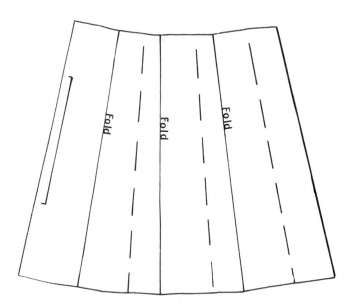

35

pleat. If desired, part of the pleat may be top stitched as shown in *figure 37*. The top stitching is worked from the right side of the fabric very close to the fold. It is best to draw a guide line using tailors' chalk prior to machining. Machine from the waist line towards the hip line and use the machine needle to pivot and turn for the slanting stitches (*figure 38*). Do not finish with back stitches on fabric where the stitching is clearly obvious. Instead pull the thread through to the wrong side and knot to secure.

36

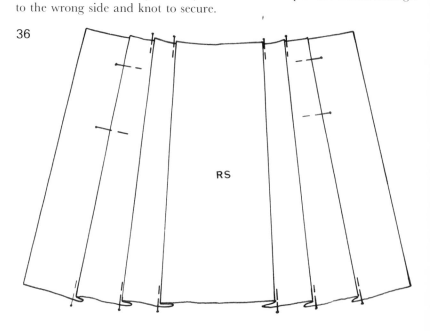

RS

37

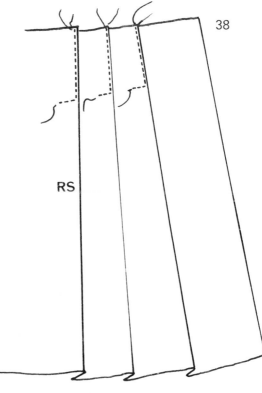

38

RS

39

39

40

Figure 39 is a ten piece pleated skirt. Here each panel forms a pleat. The pattern is as shown in *figure 40*.

Mark the pleat position and the position of the under pleat with tailors' chalk or pins on the right side of the fabric. Press the pleat fold on all ten pieces as shown in *figure 41*. Next turn the hem on each piece. The hem in *figure 39* is a top stitched hem having the raw edge neatened with zig zag (*figure 42*). Re-press the pleat at the hem position.

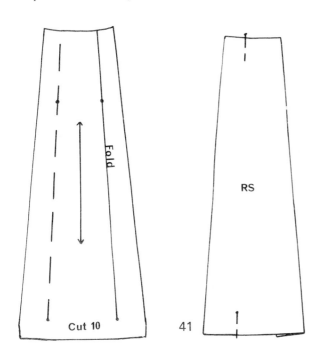

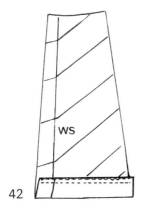

Now machine the pieces with right sides together arranging them in such a way that the pleats overlap the under pleats (*figure 43*). Stitch the seam with straight stitch and neaten together with zig zag. Machine from the waist line towards the hip to the marked position along the fold (approx 6 in. [15 cm]) to hold the top of the pleat securely in position (*figure 44*). Leave one seam open at the waist for a placket. It is very convenient to use a velcro placket in this style of skirt.

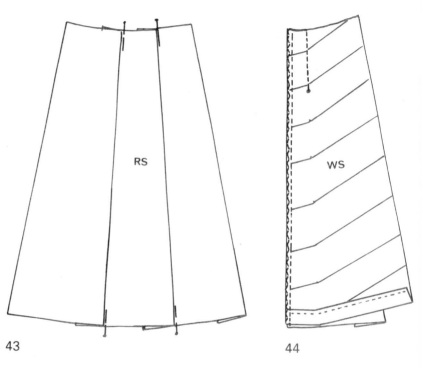

43

44

5 Pockets

As well as being functional, pockets can be used to good effect on a garment as a design feature. The size, shape and position of pockets vary according to fashion but the principles involved in making them change very little.

Side seam pocket

The side seam pocket is probably the one most commonly used to serve a practical rather than a design purpose since it is almost inconspicuous (*figure 126a*).

The pocket piece of the garment may form part of the back and front of the garment. However, very often, in order to cut the garment economically the pockets are cut separately as shown in *figure 45*. In this case the first step is to attach the pocket pieces to the appropriate side seams. It is advisable to iron on an interlining strip at the pocket position. This should be $\frac{1}{2}$ in. (1·2 cm) longer at each end of the pocket.

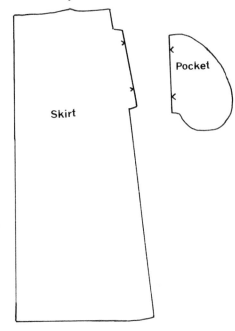

Skirt

Pocket

45

Place right sides together with notches matching and pin and machine as shown in *figure 46*. Press seams towards the pocket piece and neaten the edges with zig zag (*figure 47*).

Machine stitch the back to the front at side seams leaving the pocket area open as in *figure 48*. Reinforce the stitching with satin stitch within the seam allowance as shown. This strengthens what would otherwise be a weak spot. To complete the pocket, machine around the edge of the pocket bag (*figure 49*). Turn the pocket towards the front and press in position.

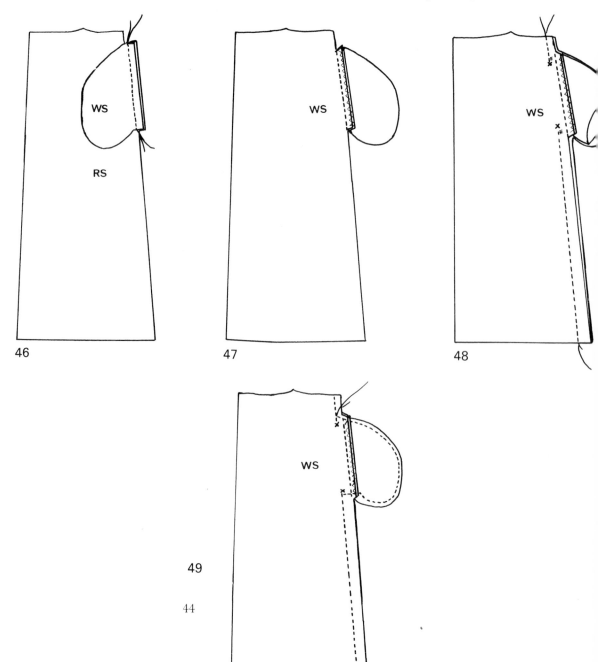

46

47

48

49

Simple patch pocket *(figure 51)*

Patch pockets are usually placed in a fairly prominent position on a garment and so it is important to ensure that they are stitched onto the garment correctly. If two pockets are used these must balance each other.

First iron on an interlining to the wrong side of the pocket piece. This is particularly important if the pocket is cut on the bias as a design feature. After ironing on the interlining, press a $\frac{1}{2}$ in. (1·2 cm) turning around the sides and lower edge of the pocket. Neaten the top edge with a medium-width zig zag stitch and then press a 1 in. (2·5 cm) turning across the top. Machine stitch around the pocket approximately $\frac{1}{4}$ in. (5 mm) from the fold of the sides and lower edge and $\frac{3}{4}$ in. (2 cm) from the top edge (*figure 50*). If you have a curved edge to the pocket you may find it easier to turn and obtain a better curve if you cut into the seam at intervals.

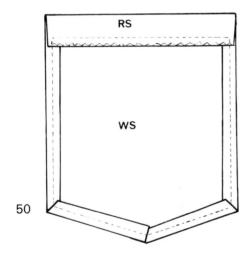

50

Now pin the pocket into position on the garment. When you are sure that the pockets are securely held in the correct position, machine stitch round the pocket. The machine stitching may be carried out in various ways. You may choose to sew exactly over the original stitching of the pocket making a bold stitching line or you may stitch as close to the fold edge as possible. Two rows of stitching worked exactly parallel by using the twin needle also makes an interesting finish. One of the needles should line up exactly with the original machining if this method is used.

Strengthening the top of the pocket is essential and this is best carried out by a small satin stitch bar.

Welt pocket

It is necessary to use an interlining in the welt especially when the fabric is cut on the bias as in *figure 51*. It is also advisable to reinforce the area of the garment at the pocket position by ironing a piece of interlining onto the wrong side (*figure 52*). To make the welt iron on the interfacing to half the width as shown in *figure 53*. Fold lengthwise with right sides together and machine stitch the ends (*figure 54*). Turn and press. Place the raw edges of the welt to the marked pocket position on the garment. The right side of the welt should be placed to the right side of the garment. The interlined half being the top half. Machine the welt into position as in *figure 55*.

51

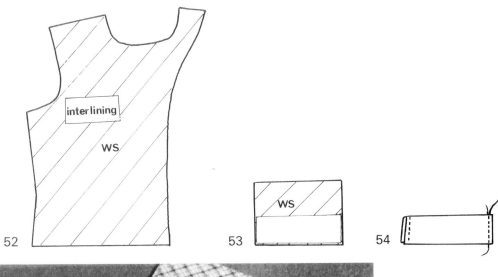

52   53   54

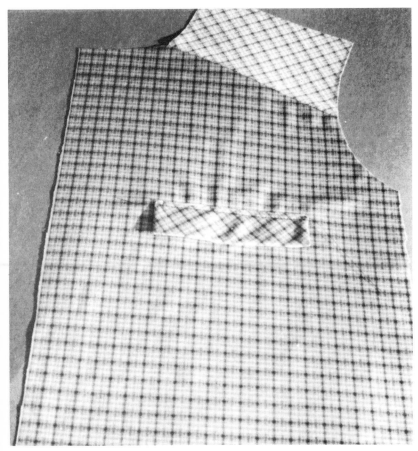

Place the pocket bags in position. The lower bag covering the welt with the raw edges together and the wrong side uppermost. Machine the bag onto the garment as shown in *figure 56*. Turn the garment to the wrong side and cut an opening between the machine stitching. Snip diagonally into the corners as shown in *figure 57*. Take the pocket bag through the opening to the wrong side of the garment (*figure 58*). Pin and machine the pocket bag catching the clipped corners securely onto the pocket bag with forward and reverse stitching (*figure 59*). Neaten the pocket bag with zig zag stitch. Press the welt up and machine stitch into position on the right side of the garment. Secure with back stitching to strengthen the part of the pocket liable to the most strain.

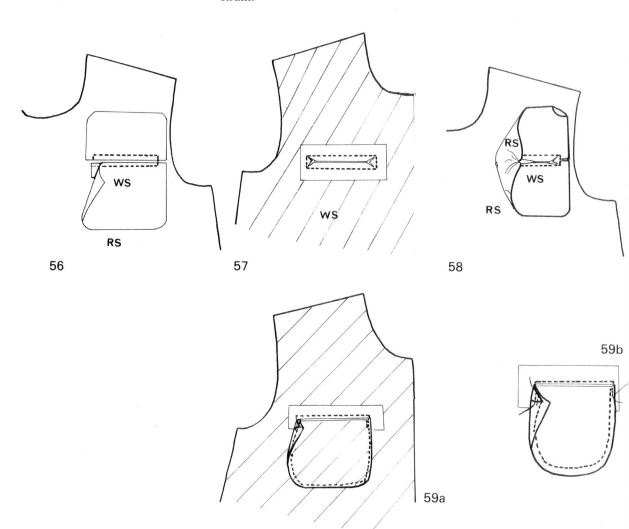

56

57

58

59b

59a

48

Faced pocket (*figure 60*)

A faced pocket is usually used in a skirt or trousers. The pattern pieces for this style of pocket comprise: the main skirt or trouser with a shaped side (*figure 61a*); a pocket facing (*figure 61b*) and a side front which also forms part of the pocket bag (*figure 61c*).

60

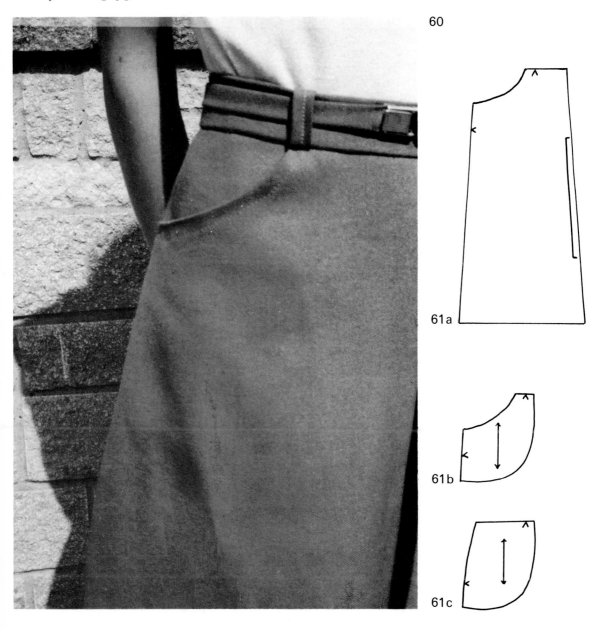

61a

61b

61c

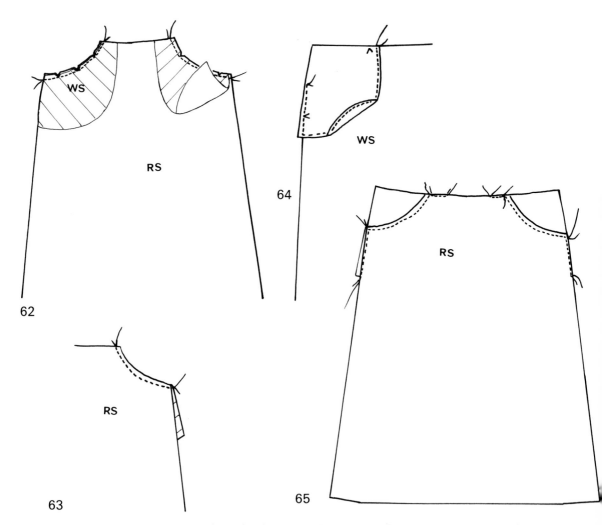

First take the pocket facings and place these on the main skirt with right sides together matching the notches. Pin and machine stitch along the pocket edge taking great care not to stretch a curved edge. On a loosely woven fabric it is advisable to iron an interlining onto the wrong side of the fabric at the position of the curve. Turn the pocket facing to the wrong side of the garment (*figure 62*). It is sometimes helpful to snip into the seam before turning to ensure that a flat seam is obtained. Top stitch the pocket edge at this stage if desired (*figure 63*).

With right sides together pin the side front to the pocket facing with notches matching. Machine the pocket edges together and neaten the edge with zig zag stitch (*figure 64*).

Stitch the pocket to the side skirt to hold this firmly in position until such time as the side seam of the garment is machined. This stitching should be made within the seam allowance (*figure 65*).

See-through pocket

Although the pocket in *figure 114* looks very much like a patch pocket its construction is slightly different. Because an open weave fabric has been used, the edges of the pocket have been enclosed in the seams. This hides the raw edge of the pocket which would otherwise show through the open weave fabric. For the lower edge of the pocket I have used the selvedge of this particular fabric. Alternatively the lower edge may be bound with a strip of the main skirt fabric to neaten the edge.

To make the flap for the pocket cut a piece of fabric $2\frac{1}{2}$ in. (6·4 cm) wide by the length of the pocket top. Fold the strip lengthwise with right side outside. Stitch the flap to the wrong side of the pocket top and neaten with zig zag. Now press the flap over to the right side of the pocket enclosing the seam (*figure 66*).

Pin the pocket into position on the skirt panel and stitch across the lower part of the pocket (*figure 67*). Machine tack the sides of the pocket and remove the pins. Pin and machine the front and side panel and the side and back seams enclosing the sides of the pocket in the seams as shown in *figure 114*.

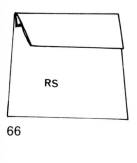

RS

66

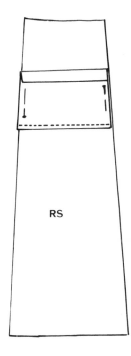

RS

67

6 Necklines

Necklines may be cut to various shapes and faced, piped, bound or collared. The main rule to remember is that whichever design is used the garment must pass over the head. Therefore, the neck edge must either be shaped out to allow for this or an opening of some kind is required.

Facings

The neckline of the dress in *figure 68* has a front and back facing seamed at the shoulder area. It is desirable in most cases to strengthen the facings by ironing on a light-weight interlining. This may not however be necessary if you are working with a closely woven firm fabric. The main reason for using an interlining is to control the stretch of the fabric and to retain the correct shape as it is stitched around the neckline. If the material is firm enough to make an interlining unnecessary there is no point in adding to the bulk around the neck by using one. Furthermore if you are using a fairly heavy fabric for your garment you may find it is better to use an alternative fabric such as lining or plain woven cotton for the facings.

Matching notches and with right sides together join the shoulder seams of the garment. Also join the shoulder seam of the facings. Open the seams and lay the facing over the garment with right sides together.

Pin around the neckline and using tailors' chalk draw a line to the desired length of the opening as shown by a broken line in *figure 69*.

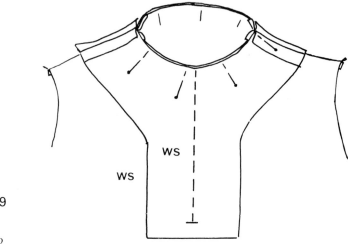

69

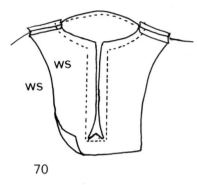

Machine around the neckline allowing the correct seam allowance. Start the stitching at one shoulder seam and work around until you almost reach the centre front. Stop stitching a $\frac{1}{4}$ in. (5 mm) away from the tailors' chalk line and using the machine needle as a pivot turn the garment to enable you to machine along the side of the centre front line.

Stitch to the marked length of the line using the right side of the presser foot as a guide along the chalk line. At the end of the line pivot again, work about four stitches, and turn to continue along the other side of the line and round the remaining part of the neckline.

Trim away excessive seam allowance and cut a slit along the chalk line of the centre front, snipping into the corners as shown in *figure 70*. To enable the facing to lie flat when turned you may need to snip the curved edge towards the seam.

Turn the facing to the wrong side and press on the wrong side pulling the facing inwards so that the seam is only visible on the wrong side of the garment. Top stitch if desired from the right side. This gives an opportunity to use one of the patterned stitches if your machine has such a facility.

Flat collar (*figure 71*)

A flat collar may be stitched onto the neckline using the front facing to neaten the front neck edge. The back neck edge may be finished with zig zag stitch avoiding the use of a back neck facing. Facings do tend to be bulky and I do try to avoid using them whenever possible.

71

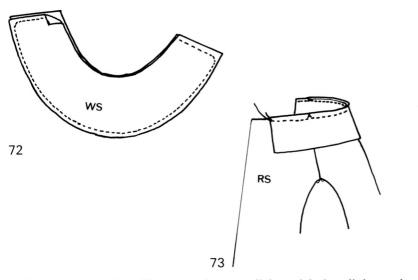

WS

72

RS

73

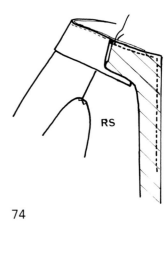

RS

74

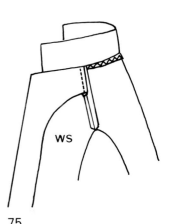

WS

75

First make the collar. If necessary iron on a light-weight interlining to the under collar. If both top and under collar pieces are the same, only use interlining on one piece and make sure this piece is stitched adjacent to the neck edge when you come to attach the collar. Whether or not an interlining is necessary depends on the type of fabric being used. This is explained in the section dealing with facings on page 52.

Pin the collar with the right sides together and machine round the outer edge of the collar. At the corners of a collar it is best to make one or two stitches in a diagonal direction to achieve a smooth seam when turning the collar (*figure 72*). One diagonal stitch is sufficient for a fine soft fabric but two or three stitches should be used for thicker fabrics. Control the drive wheel by hand when making these stitches. The machine needle in its lowest position should be used as a pivot when turning the corners. Trim excess fabric from the seams. Turn and press the collar with the seam towards the under-side making it invisible on the top collar. Find the centre back of the collar and the centre back of the garment and pin the collar into position with the right side of the garment to the right side of the under collar. Work from the centre back round to the left and right fronts pinning the collar into position at the same time matching the notches.

Now machine the collar into position, stitching in the centre of the seam allowance (*figure 73*). Place the front facing in position enclosing the front collar between the garment and the facing (*figure 74*).

The right side of the facing should be to the right side of the garment. Pin and machine the facing to the garment securing the collar in place. Take the correct seam allowance and machine all ʾund the neck edge from left front to right front. Turn the facing and turn a small hem across the shoulder area. Machine this to the shoulder seam along the channel of machine stitching. Neaten the back neck edge with zig zag stitch (*figure 75*).

55

Shirt or stand collar without facing (*figures 37 and 51*)

Use an interlining as necessary and make the collar in the same way as described for a flat collar. Pin the top and under collar with right sides together and machine stitch from the notches leaving the seam allowance on the neck edge free (*figure 76*). Now pin the under collar neck edge to the neck edge of the garment with the right sides together. To do this you must separate the two collar pieces at the neck edge. Machine the under collar to the garment along the seam line as shown in *figure 77*.

    Now bring the top collar over to the inside of the garment. Turn a hem at the neck edge of the collar, pin into position over the seam and machine stitch as shown in *figure 78*.

    Figure 79 shows the finished collar from the wrong side of the garment.

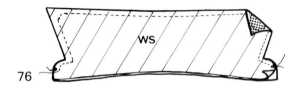

76

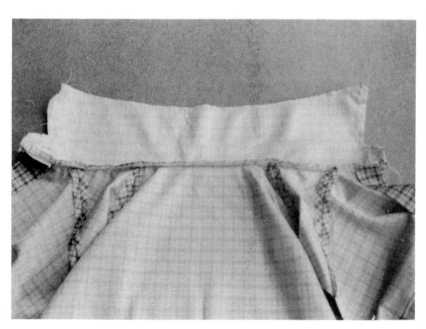

77

56

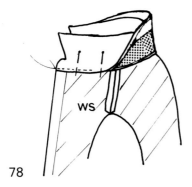

78

79

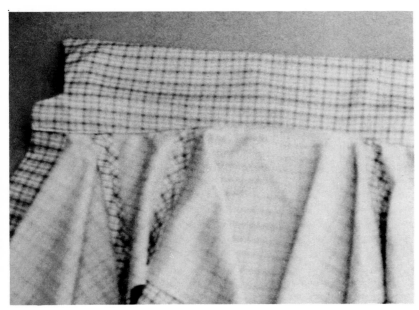

Bound neckline (*figure 80*)

A bound neckline does not take away any of the fabric in seams. The neck edge, therefore, must be the correct fitting shape before you begin to bind it. The bound neckline requires a strip of fabric cut on the bias about $1\frac{1}{4}$ in (3 cm) wide. To find the true bias, turn over a corner of the fabric so that the warp and weft threads run parallel to each other. The selvedge forms a right angle (*figure 81*).

80

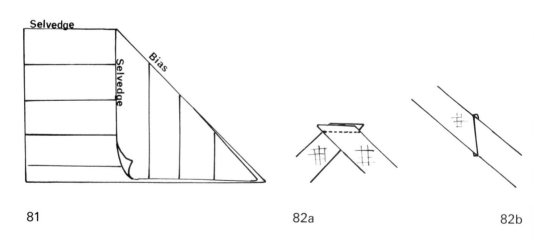

81

82a

82b

Cut along the fold and cut the required strips parallel to this first cut. If it is necessary to make a join in the strips, pin these with right sides together and stitch on the straight grain (*figure 82a*), press the seam open and trim off edges (*figure 82b*). Always try to avoid using a joined strip with the join in an obvious position i.e. centre front area of a neckline.

Neaten one edge of the bias strip. Neaten either by small zig zag stitching or a very narrow straight-stitched turning. Machine the raw edge of the strip to the neck edge of the garment with right sides together taking about $\frac{3}{8}$ in. (1 cm) seam allowance. Stretch the bias strip very slightly around the curved edge of the front neck (*figure 83*). Trim away a little of the bias seam if a heavy fabric is being used.

Now press the binding towards the seam and over to the inside of the garment. Pin the neatened edge so that it overlaps the seam line. Pin from the right side. Now top stitch from the right side, stitching as close to the edge of the binding as possible with a matching thread (*figure 84*). The stitching becomes inconspicuous as the binding rolls back over this in wear.

The bias strip may be used in place of a shaped facing. Stitch the bias strip to the right side of the fabric as shown in *figure 83*. Instead of binding the neck edge as in *figure 84* the bias strip may be pressed to the wrong side along the stitching line. Because of the extra give available with a bias-cut piece of fabric, it is possible to top stitch the lower edge stretching it to the required length (*figure 85*).

This method of facing is used for the dress in *figure 126b*.

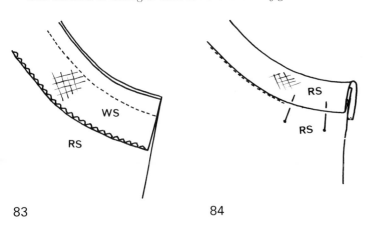

83   84

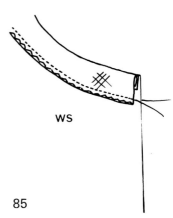

85

7 Sleeves

Set in sleeves

The generally accepted definition of a set in sleeve is one which is stitched into a garment around the natural armhole area of the bodice. The sleeve is always larger than the armhole to allow for fitting around the upper arm. The sleeve may be stitched to the bodice either on the flat with only the shoulder seam of the garment stitched, or on the round where the sleeve and bodice seams have been previously stitched.

The flat method has gained great favour recently and is frequently used in the clothing industry for blouses and summer weight dresses. A machinist is able to feed the garment through the machine in a less cluttered manner.

Pin and machine the shoulder seams of the garment first with the right sides together. Pin the sleeve to the garment armhole area with the right sides together matching the notches. The crown of the sleeve should match the shoulder seam. Pin at regular intervals easing away the fullness of the sleevehead. I do not like to use a gathering thread as suggested with so many commercial patterns. The aim of a nicely set sleeve is to stitch the sleeve with a smooth seam. No tucks should be in evidence unless of course the style you are making has a puff or gathered sleeve. Ensure that the right sleeve is in the right armhole and the left in the left. Machine these with the sleeve uppermost. Take in the correct seam allowance and ease the fabric under the presser foot. Flatten the sleeve head with your hands close to the presser foot. It is surprisingly easy to ease away quite an amount of fabric without tucks by this method. It is worthwhile practising this in your spare time to improve your skill in handling various fabrics. Trim the seam if necessary and zig zag the raw edges together. Press the seam towards the sleeve (*figure 86a*).

With the right sides together, pin the side seams and the sleeve seams and machine stitch these (*figure 86b*). Neaten the raw edges together with zig zag stitch or press open and neaten these singly.

The round method is an alternative way of making a set in sleeve. Stitch the shoulder seams and side seams of the garment. Machine the underarm seam of the sleeve. A wrist length sleeve will necessitate the easing away of fullness around the elbow area. Sometimes a small dart is suggested for this area. I personally do not care to use a dart at the elbow and advise against this because of its rather ugly appearance. Instead I ease away the fullness allowed for the dart over a distance of approximately 3 in. (7·6 cm). This still allows for the necessary fullness around the back elbow area.

86a

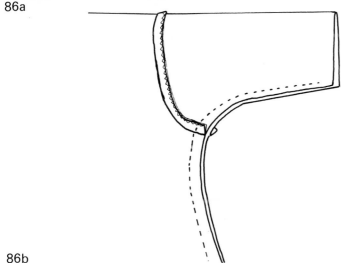

86b

Hold the garment with the wrong side uppermost and pass the sleeve, with the right side out, through the armhole. Pin the sleeve head to the shoulder seam with right sides together. Insert pins at the under arm seams and the notches to secure the sleeve to the bodice. Be sure to have the correct sleeve in the correct side of the garment. It is so easy to make mistakes especially when using plain fabric. Do check that the notches match and that the right sides of the fabric are together.

61

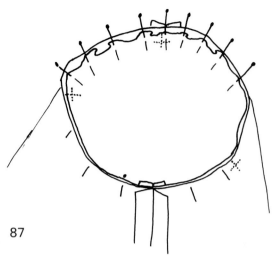

87

Pin at regular intervals between the notches and shoulder seam distributing the ease evenly as shown in *figure 87*. With the sleeve uppermost machine the sleeve into the armhole taking the correct seam allowance. Flatten the sleeve head with your hands close to the presser foot to ensure that no tucks are made (*figure 88*). Neaten the raw edges together with zig zag stitch and press towards the sleeve.

Cap sleeve

The cap sleeve in *figure 126b* is simply hemmed and turned back to form a cuff. To make this, first join the shoulder seams. Then make a hem at the armhole position. This may be wider at the shoulder than the underarm position (*figure 89*). Machine the hem using straight stitch. Now turn the fold of the hem to the right side over the stitches to make the cuff. Press into position. Join the side seams and neaten (*figure 90*).

If desired, the side seams may be joined at the same time as the shoulder seams before the sleeve hem is made. However, it is not quite so easy to hem when both seams are joined.

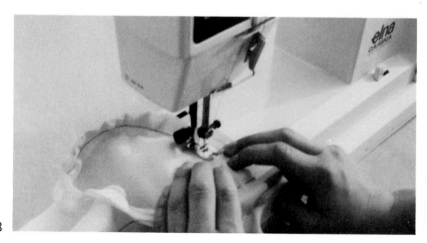

88

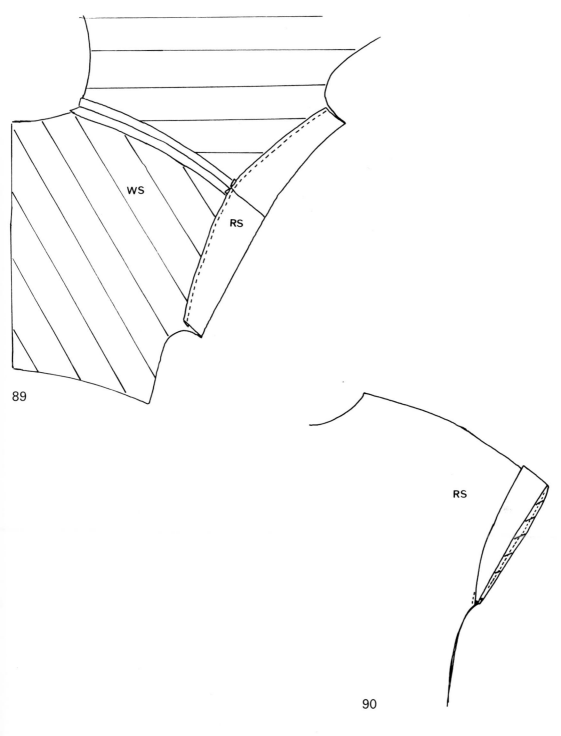

WS

RS

89

RS

90

8 Fasteners and openings

Buttonholes and buttons

Before the zig zag machine was designed the method of working buttonholes was to hand work around the slit using buttonhole or blanket stitch. To use the sewing machine for buttonholes the dressmaker had to make a bound or piped buttonhole which was very obvious and often unsightly. Now buttonholes can be made using satin stitch on a basic zig zag machine or the automatic buttonholer on the more sophisticated machines. These make good strong inconspicuous buttonholes.

Whichever method is used you must first mark the position of the buttonholes onto the right front of the garment. Remember that the button shank or fish eye will rest at the end of the buttonhole which is nearest to the edge of the garment, and that when the button is fastened there should be some clearance between the button and the front edge of the garment. Don't guess at the buttonhole positions – work them out with the aid of a tape measure. The start of the buttonhole needs to be positioned almost the same distance from the front edge of the garment as the diameter of the intended button. This will ensure that when the button is fastened half the button will overlap the buttonhole and there will be a clearance the size of half a button. This achieves a good balance. The length of the buttonhole needs to be the size of the button plus an allowance for ease of fastening. The ease allowance will vary according to the thickness of the button. Generally an allowance of $\frac{1}{8}$ in. (2 mm) should be sufficient but for thicker buttons it is advisable to allow the thickness of the button and add this to the $\frac{1}{8}$ in. (2 mm) when working out the overall required buttonhole size. A machine-made buttonhole has two parallel rows of satin stitching and a bar tack at each end. The buttonhole is worked prior to the slash being made between the two rows of satin stitch.

It is possible to make a very acceptable buttonhole on most zig zag machines without the necessity of turning the fabric, provided that your machine has three needle positions. Trying to turn a garment under the machine can be a very daunting procedure and often the buttonhole made is not very satisfactory. It is helpful to use a buttonhole foot which has grooves on the underside allowing the raised stitches of the buttonhole to pass easily underneath. If you do not have a buttonhole foot enquire at your local machine supplier. These are available for most makes of machine and are a very worthwhile investment.

To start, replace the general purpose presser foot with the grooved buttonhole foot. The buttonhole is worked in four stages.

Stage 1
Set the stitch length at between 0 and 1. Position the needle to the left. Adjust the stitch width to zig zag 2. Work the left side of the buttonhole to the desired length previously marked with tailors' chalk. Raise the needle, but not the presser foot.

Stage 2
Move the needle from the left to the centre position. Change the stitch width setting to 4 or the widest zig zag. Work a bar of about four stitches.

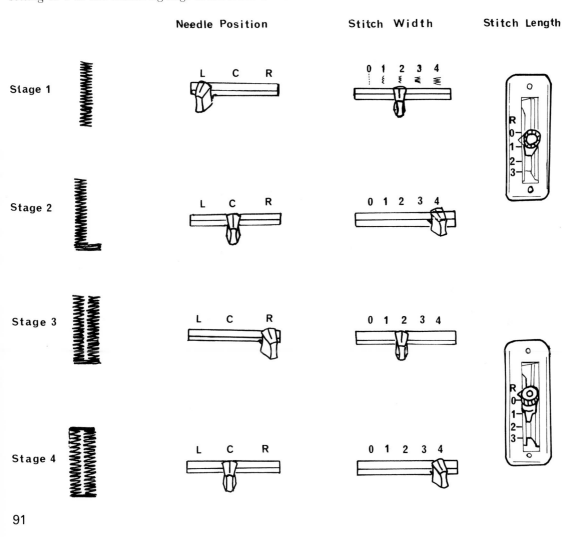

91

Stage 3

Alter the raised needle from the centre to the right position. Change back to a stitch width at almost 2. This is to provide a cutting space. Put the machine into the reverse stitch position just below 0 and work the right side of the buttonhole. The grooves in the buttonhole foot will guide the foot over the left side of the satin stitch.

Stage 4

This completes the final bar tack. Position the raised needle to the centre point. The stitch width should be at the widest zig zag position and the stitch length should be changed to 0. Work a strong bar of about six stitches to finish off.

The chart in *figure 91* shows the various machine settings for each stage of the buttonhole.

The principle involved with an automatic buttonhole is similar in that the buttonhole is worked in four stages. Sometimes there is a fifth programme used to finish off the buttonhole more securely. With an automatic buttonholer you set the stitch selector dial on buttonhole and instead of

92

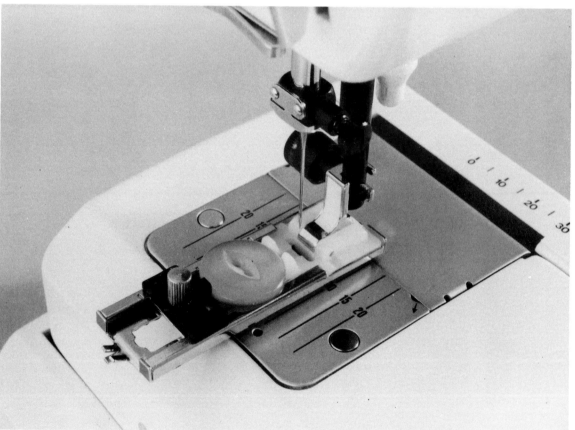

having to adjust the needle position, zig zag width and stitch length yourself these are adjusted automatically by turning to the appropriate number.

Set the dial at 1 for the first row of satin stitch to be worked. Having worked the first row to the required length the dial should be turned to 2. The controls are now set automatically for the working of the bar. Turning the dial to 3 will put the machine in reverse and adjust the satin stitch width to enable you to work the right side of the buttonhole. Stage four is the final bar. If the dial has a fifth point this is usually a straight stitch and it is intended that only three or four stitches be made to finish off the work.

There are various attachments available to help you achieve really superb buttonholes. Some of the attachments fit onto the buttonhole foot and are supplied with the machine while others are offered as optional extras. The measuring device shown in *figure 92* is extremely useful in that it may be set to the size of the button and has the allowance for ease included. Once set to the correct size the button is removed and the guide is there to ensure that all the buttonholes are the same size. *Figure 93* shows the same attachment which has the facility for holding a buttonhole cord to achieve a stronger, more tailored buttonhole. It may be that there is an attachment to suit your needs—ask at your local machine shop to find out what is new!

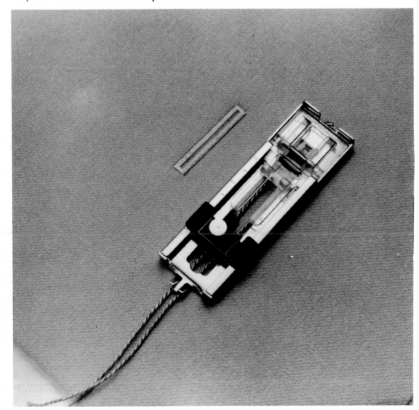

93

There are attachments available to aid in sewing on buttons by machine. Shank buttons are not suitable for machine stitching since the machine needle can only penetrate from the top of a button. Although I advocate using the sewing machine for as many tasks as possible, I do believe that unless you have many buttons to sew on it is as well to sew them on by hand. Personally I like to relax in an easy chair to carry out this final operation in making a garment.

Snap fasteners

A popular alternative to buttons and buttonholes is to use snap fasteners as on the jacket in *figure 94*. These snap fasteners require no sewing and are applied by the use of special pliers which can be seen in *figure 122*. Full instructions for applying these are given with the snap fasteners which are obtainable in several different finishes.

Zip fasteners

A zip fastener is probably the most popular way of finishing an opening. These may be machined into a seam in numerous ways. They may be sewn from the right side or wrong side of the garment with the zip teeth open or closed according to personal choice. Whichever choice is made a zipper foot attachment is extremely useful. The zipper foot shown in *figure 95* is placed on a sliding bar to enable stitching to be machined on either side. The advantage of a zipper foot is that the needle is able to penetrate the fabric closer to the teeth of the zip than would be the case with a normal presser foot. *Figure 95* illustrates the method of inserting a zip fastener with the teeth open. The seam has been pressed open making a good fold edge. Pin the zip into position with the fold to the edge of the open teeth. Pins must be at right angles to the fold. Machine almost to the end of the zip. Lower the needle into the cloth to secure the garment whilst you lift the presser foot lever. Pull the zip into a closed position to pass the needle. Lower the presser foot and continue to machine to the end of a zip. Cross over the end of the zip tape using the machine needle as a pivot while turning. Make a few stitches along the other side of the zip while the teeth remain closed. Then open the teeth using the needle of the machine to hold the work as before. Continue to machine the open zip to the end as shown in *figure 95*. When the zip fastener is closed the fold edges should meet together hiding the teeth from sight.

Some people do experience difficulty when inserting zip fasteners and find that despite using a zipper foot the teeth of the zip still show when the stitching is completed.

Stitching the zip from the wrong side with the seam temporarily tacked together may solve the problem. To use this method machine the seams in the usual way and back stitch to secure. Alter the upper tension and machine tack the opening as a temporary measure. Do not back stitch the tacking stitches (*figure 96*). Press the seam open. Pin the zip into position with the centre of the

68

94

95

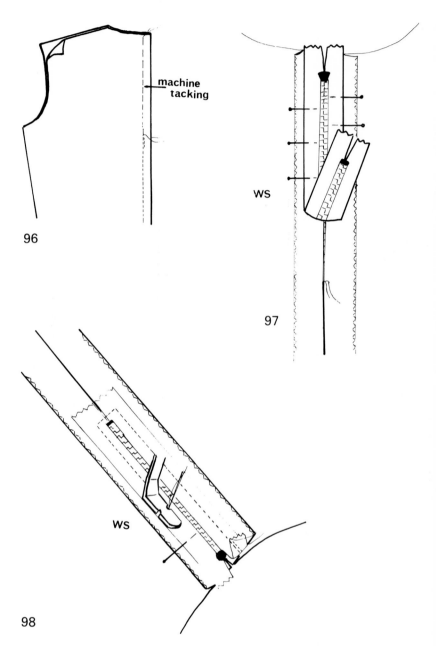

96

machine
tacking

97

WS

WS

98

teeth over the tacked seam (*figure 97*). Machine from the wrong side at a position almost central to the zip tape shown in *figure 98*. Start and finish with back stitches to secure the machining. Simply pull out the temporary machine tacking and press. By working on the wrong side you will avoid stretching the fabric which is so often the cause of a wavy effect around the zip area.

70

Placket opening

The front placket opening is a popular feature for dresses and shirts with or without a collar (*figures 37 and 126b*).

To make this placket mark a line on the right side of the fabric to the left of the centre front (*figure 99*). Note that as your front bodice is in front of you on the table with the right side of the fabric uppermost, so the left side of the garment is to your right. The line must be as long as the desired opening. The reason for this line being made off centre is to ensure that the buttons on the finished placket are central. The line therefore should be approximately $\frac{3}{4}$ in. (2 cm) from the centre front. Cut a strip of fabric 2 in. (5 cm) wide by twice the length of the line plus 1 in. (2·5 cm). Cut a slit along this line. Fold the strip of fabric lengthwise with the wrong side inside and press. Pin and machine the strip of fabric with the raw edges along the slit with right sides of the fabric together. Machine quite close to the raw edge – no more than $\frac{1}{4}$ in. (5 mm) (*figure 100*). At the end of the slit work two stitches across before turning to stitch the other side (*figure 101*). To neaten and at the same time strengthen

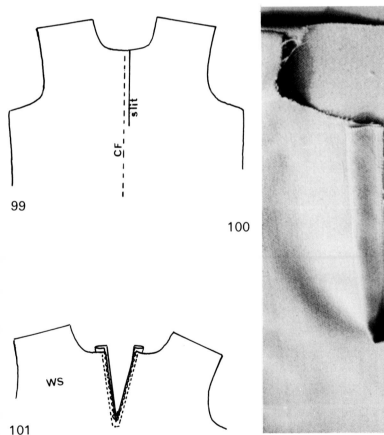

99

100

101

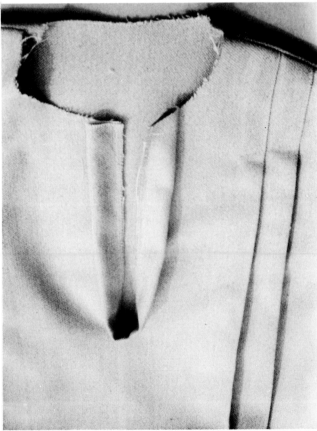

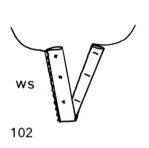

WS

102

103

the edges machine with zig zag stitch as shown. Now pass the strip of fabric through to the wrong side of the garment. Arrange the folded piece of fabric to serve as a placket extension on the left side of the garment and a facing on the right side of the opening.

Sew buttons onto the extension piece and make the buttonholes on the right side as shown in *figure 102*.

A sleeve opening at cuff (*figure 103*) employs the same principle as described above. Here the strip is narrower, about 1 in. (2·5 cm) wide. Mark the position of the slit which should be towards the back of the sleeve and proceed as before (*figure 104*).

The cuff is made and stitched using the same technique as that described below for the skirt waist band.

104

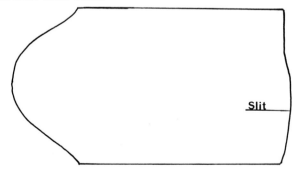

Slit

Velcro placket

Inserting velcro into the skirt side seam is an easy and very good way of making a placket.

You will need to extend the side seam at the left side for the area of the velcro. *Figure 105a* shows the seam allowance extended by 1 in. (2·5 cm) to a depth of about 8 in. (20 cm).

Cut a piece of velcro 7 in. (18 cm) long and separate the two strips. You will notice that one strip is soft and the other firm. Use the firm strip for the front piece of the skirt and the soft for the back. This way the soft piece will lie closest to the body. Pin and machine the velcro strips to the right side of the fabric at the extension position (*figures 105b and 105c*). Pin and machine the side seam with right sides of the fabric together. Fasten the velcro at the extension (*figure 106*).

Snip the back seam allowance just below the extension. Open the lower part of the side seam and press the extension towards the front as shown in *figure 107*. The extension piece of the front skirt is now folded under forming a facing with the velcro stitched into the correct position to fasten the placket.

Top stitch the front facing along the fold to hold this firm (*figures 108 and 112*).

If you use velcro on a washable garment, always fasten the velcro together before washing, to avoid picking up fluff from other clothes onto the hooks of the velcro.

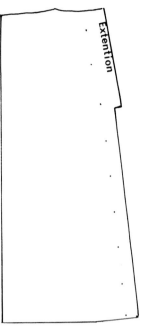

105a

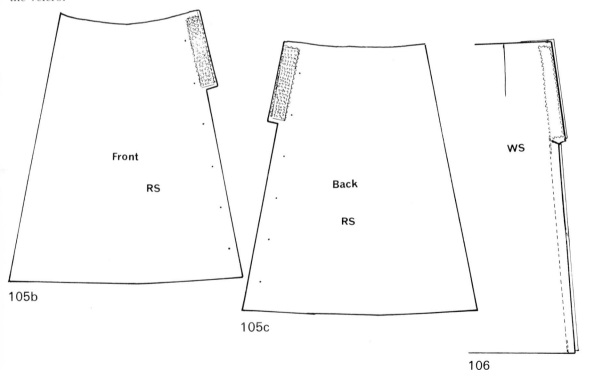

105b

Front

RS

105c

Back

RS

WS

106

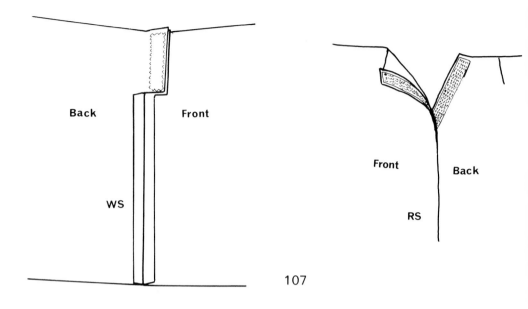

Back   Front

WS

107

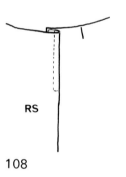

RS

108

Front   Back

RS

Skirt waist band

Cut the waist band to measure the same as the skirt waist plus the placket extension and seam allowances. Iron a fine interlining on to the wrong side of the waist band or stitch a stronger interlining to half of the waist band as in *figure 109*.

With right sides together pin and machine the waist band to the skirt allowing the waist band to overlap the opening and extension by the width of the seam allowance (*figure 110*). Press the waist band upwards. When you wish to make the waist fastening less obvious it is a good idea to use a strong snap fastener. Special pliers are available for use with these snap fasteners. Insert the stud part of the fastener in the waist band at this stage. Position the stud at the side front position of the skirt band 1 in (2·5 mm) from the end. The stud should be on the right side of the fabric with the pronged ring piece on the interfacing (*figure 111*).

Neaten the edge of the facing with zig zag stitch. Fold the band with right sides together and machine the ends taking $\frac{1}{2}$ in. (1 cm) seams (*figure 112*). Turn the right side out and press the waist band into position. Hold the inside edge of the waist band so that it overlaps the waist seam. Pin from the front side at regular intervals. Now top stitch the waist band firmly into position. The needle should penetrate just under the waist seam, making the stitching inconspicuous (*figure 113*).

A very easy way to make a waist band is to use the $\frac{3}{4}$ in. (2 cm) wide shirring elastic tape. This comprises seven strands of shirring elastic held together with nylon webbing (*figure 114*).

74

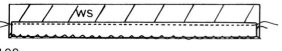

109

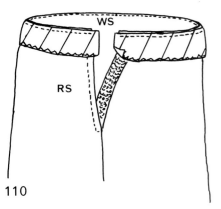

110

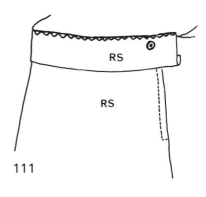

111

114

113

    Cut a strip of fabric for the waist band 3 in. (7·5 cm) wide and long enough
to pass comfortably over the hips. Join the band across the width with right
side together. Fold the band in half lengthwise with the wrong side inside and
press, enclosing the seam. Find the half and quarter positions of the skirt and
waist band. Using the one stage gathering method described in Chapter 4 join
the skirt to the waist band. Neaten the raw edge with zig zag stitch. Now find
the half and quarter positions of the elastic and the waist band. Pin the elastic
to the waist band at these positions. Starting with back stitches, stitch the
elastic to the waist band stretching the elastic to fit. Machine three or four
rows of straight stitching across the nylon webbing. Overlap the ends of the
elastic to make a good flat join. Be sure to avoid catching the waist band seam
under the elastic tape.

9 Knitwear

The sweaters in *figure 115* are made on an ordinary domestic sewing machine using only the basic zig zag stitch.

Material suitable for sweat shirts is now obtainable in department stores but knitted fabric similar to that used in the photograph is not so readily available. However, it can sometimes be found in shops selling remnants or on market stalls in hosiery manufacturing districts.

It is first necessary to make a pattern. Take this from a ready-made

115

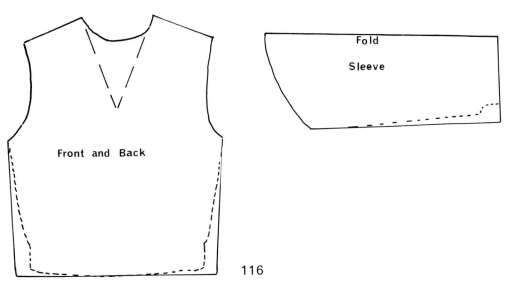

116

sweater. Turn the ready-made garment inside out and draw around the back of it. Use a tracing wheel through the armhole seam the take a copy of the outline. Outline the sleeve with the top sleeve adjacent to a folded piece of paper – this way you trace off the back and front sleeve together. Do not make the mistake of shaping your pattern into the rib, as shown with a broken line, but cut the side seam straight. The front of the sweater may be cut exactly the same as the back except for the V neck shaping (*figure 116*).

After cutting the fabric work quickly handling the cloth as little as possible. Be careful not to stretch the raw edges so causing the knitting to ladder.

With right sides together join the shoulder seams. Take a very small seam allowance (not more than $\frac{1}{4}$ in. [5 mm]) and machine using zig zag stitch width 1 and stitch length 2. Adjust the needle position to the right if necessary to achieve a narrow seam. The reason for using zig zag stitch rather than a straight stitch is to allow for some stretch in the seam. Now stitch over the seam again, this time using zig zag stitch width 3 and stitch length 1. This reinforces the seam and neatens the raw edge. Ease the seam under the presser foot so as not to stretch it.

Machine the sleeves in on the flat with right sides together. Use the same method of seaming as for the shoulder (*figure 117*). Join the side and sleeve seams in the same way.

The ribbing is cut from the same fabric as the sweater. It is however cut shorter than the part of the sweater it is to edge. This is how the ribbed effect is achieved.

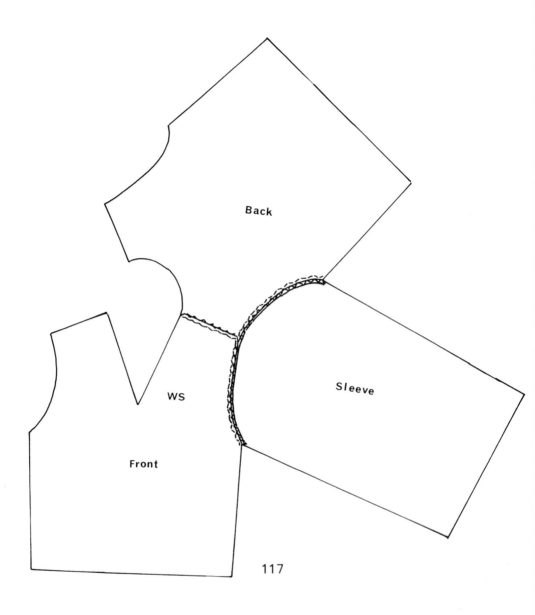

Back

WS

Front

Sleeve

117

Neck ribbing

Measure the total neck circumference after the shoulder seams have been joined. Cut a strip of fabric $2\frac{1}{4}$ in. (6 cm) wide. The length should be about 1–2 in. (2·5–5 cm) less than the sweater neck circumference. For the front mitre fold the strip in half with right sides together and cut a V $1\frac{1}{4}$ in. (3 cm) deep. Machine along the edges of the V as shown in *figure 118a*. Fold the strip lengthwise with the wrong sides together enclosing the V to make the mitre. Pin and machine the outer edges at the front to hold this firm (*figure 118b*).

Find the centre back of the sweater and the neck ribbing and pin these with right sides together. Pin the centre front of the rib to the right side of the sweater. Pin the ribbing all the way round the neck. You will find it necessary to slightly stretch the edge of the ribbing to ensure a good finished fit. It is therefore important to machine this in position as quickly as possible and to reinforce with extra machining.

Cuff ribbing

Cut the cuff ribbing 4 in. (10·2 cm) wide by a length to fit the wrist plus ease and seam allowance (approximately $8\frac{1}{2}$ in. [220 mm]). Join the strips across the width with right sides together as in *figure 118c*. Fold the cuff in half enclosing the seam as shown in *figure 118d*. Pin the cuff to the sleeve with right sides together. Match the cuff seam with the sleeve seam. It will be necessary to ease the sleeve onto the cuff. Machine the cuff to the sleeve using the same seaming method as for the rest of the sweater.

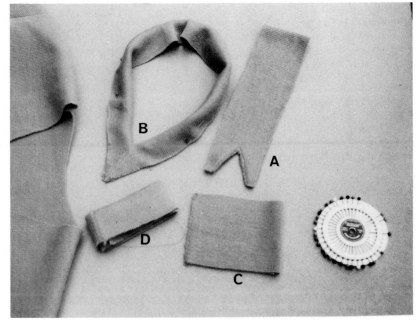

118

119

Waist ribbing

Cut the ribbing strip 5 in. (13 cm) wide. The length should be 4 in. (10 cm) to 5 in. (13 cm) shorter than the sweater waist after the side seams have been joined. Join the strip across the width and pin this to the right side of the sweater. Proceed as for the cuff, easing the sweater onto the band. *Figure 119* shows the wrong side of a sweater made on the zig zag machine.

This method of seaming may be used for stretchy knits and towelling fabrics for tee shirts, track suits and beachwear. The secret of success is in feeding the cloth through the machine without excessive stretching which causes wavy seams.

If your machine has the facility for stitching overlocked seams as in *figure 11*, then it is only necessary to machine the seams once.

The tee shirt in *figure 123* is seamed in the same way as the sweaters. The neck rib is cut $2\frac{1}{2}$ in. (6 cm) wide by 15 in. (38 cm) long and the cuffs are $2\frac{1}{2}$ in. (6 cm) by 11 in. (28 cm).

Make the neck rib and cuff rib in the same way as described for the sweater cuff *figure 118 c and d*. The ribs should then be stitched to the appropriate part taking a narrow seam with a narrow zig zag stitch. A free arm is an asset when stitching cuffs and neck ribs (*figure 120*). When the ribs have been stitched with zig zag, top stitch from the right side pressing the seam away from the rib. The overlock or double overlock stitch is ideal for this purpose, or you may like to use an alternative fancy stitch. Whichever finish you choose it must

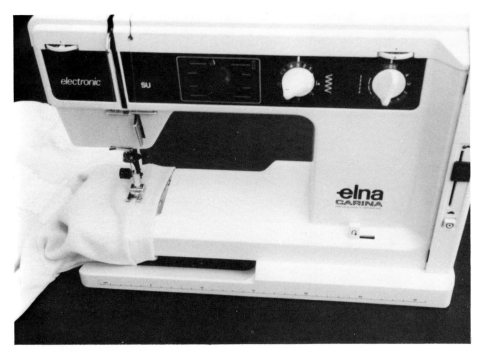

have a fair amount of 'give' because the garment has to stretch to pass over the head. If only a basic zig zag stitch is available this may be used set at a short stitch length of between 1 and 2 and a stitch width of 3.

10 Personal features

Use your zig zag machine to personalize clothing. Such features as lettering, appliqué and simple embroidery may be achieved with a basic zig zag machine. The more sophisticated machines offer numerous decorative stitches.

One or two examples of personal features have already been used in this book.

Lettering

The lettering on the sweaters (*figure 115*) is worked in simple zig zag stitch, width 2 and length between 0 and 1. In order to move the fabric freely under the needle to shape the letters the feed teeth must be put out of action. The way in which the teeth are put out of action varies with different makes of machine. Some have a plate called a darning plate which clips over the teeth, allowing the cloth to run smoothly over it. Others have a device to place beneath the needle plate raising it clear of the teeth. Alternatively the teeth may be dropped mechanically lower than the needle plate.

Replace the general purpose foot with a darning foot (*figure 121*). This foot rises and falls with the needle once the presser foot lever has been lowered. The lever at the side of the foot rests against the needle screw. As the needle penetrates the cloth the foot presses on the cloth. As the needle rises the needle screw lifts the lever which in turn lifts the foot from the work enabling the machinist to move the work freely. Lettering is really quite easy and fun to work. Try it out on scraps of fabric first. You may find it easier to use an embroidery ring to hold the fabric taut. Place the fabric under the needle, lower the foot and start to write. Run the machine at a fairly high speed and guide the material very slowly to shape the letters. You may like to write on the fabric with tailors' chalk first and follow the lines. I personally find it easier to work freehand without marked guide lines. It is really quite exciting to see the letters being worked as you guide the fabric.

When it is necessary to go over part of a letter twice move quickly along the first line and work back slowly covering the first stitches with satin stitch. It is best to work the letters of each word in a continuous flow without breaks.

The lettering on the sweaters was carried out prior to making up the garment in order to work on a flat piece of fabric. In this case the lettering area is backed by an iron on interlining to give a firmer finish.

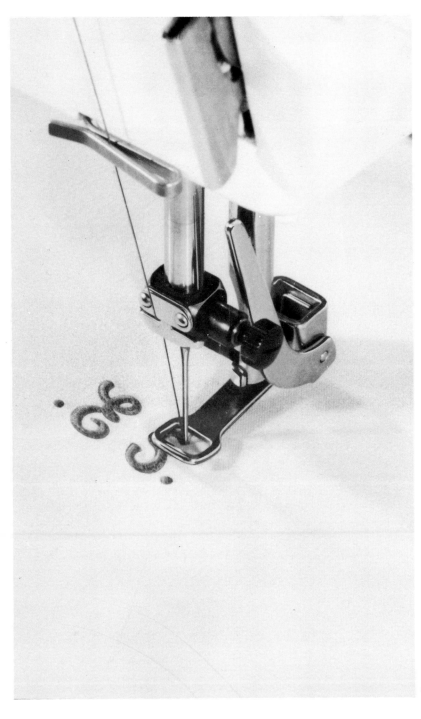

121

122

Appliqué

Very simple shapes may be applied to a garment to give an individual finish. The flowers on the jacket in *figure 94* comprise just five petal shapes and a stalk to each flower. These are cut from the same fabric as the lining. Cut the simple shapes and pin these into position. Stitch around the edge of each petal and the stalks using zig zag stitch width 2 and length 3 to secure. Now use satin stitch width 3 and length between 0 and 1 and stitch over the edge of the petals in a matching thread. If desired a bold embroidery thread may be used for greater emphasis. Reduce the width of the last few stitches at the point ends of the petals. This will allow for better shaping (*figure 122*). The appliqué work is carried out first before the garment is made up.

The tee shirt in *figure 123* has a contrasting band. The band is stitched across the front of the bodice with straight stitch immediately after cutting the garment. The band has then been edged with scallop stitch neatening the raw edge at the same time. The scallop edging adds extra interest and makes a change from satin stitch. Experiment with other stitches available with your machine.

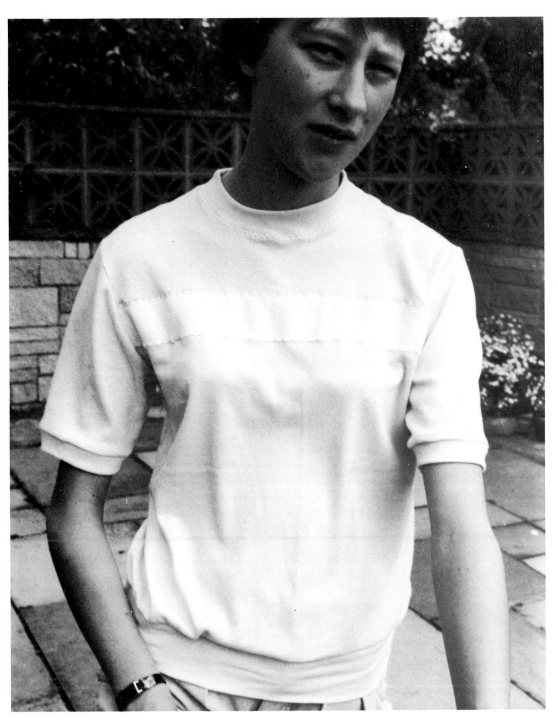

123

There are many ideas for shapes that may be used in appliqué work. Letters may be cut in contrasting fabric and applied to a garment. If you have scraps of printed fabric with distinctive shapes i.e. flowers, animals, fruit etc. these may be cut out and used on a plain fabric. Stars, sun, moon and rainbows are other popular shapes for appliqué. Choose a shape that suits the style of garment you are making but keep it simple. Remember that the appliqué is a point of interest and one soon tires of an 'over done' piece of work.

Cut away work

Petal shapes are used again in *figure 80* but this time the shapes are cut away. Draw the shapes onto the right side of the fabric using tailors' chalk. Thread the machine with the colour you require. You may wish to use a contrasting colour or a matching colour. I used a general purpose thread (Sylko supreme) in a contrasting colour – white on red fabric. Use satin stitch width 3 length between 0 and 1, and work round the chalked outline. Reduce the width of the last few stitches at the point ends of the petals. This will allow for better shaping. When all the petals have been worked, cut away the centre of each as close to the stitching as possible (*figure 124*). The petals may be arranged in an irregular way as in *figure 80* or be grouped together to form a flower in a similar way to the appliqué in *figure 94*.

Quilting

Quilting provides an interesting design feature in *figure 68*. Initially the waist panel is cut larger than the pattern piece. The panel is backed with wadding and iron-on interlining. Cut these larger than the pattern piece too. To hold the wadding firm and also ensure its smooth running over the feed teeth, iron the interlining onto the wadding. Now pin the fabric panel over the wadding with the right side of the fabric uppermost. Use the quilting foot with the guide to ensure that parallel rows of stitching are worked (*figure 125*). For a small panel as in *figure 68* work the squares about $\frac{3}{4}$ in. (2 cm) to 1 in. (2·5 cm) in size, but for larger garments i.e. jackets and waistcoats larger squares may be made. The quilting guide should be adjusted to the correct width. Work all the longest rows of stitching first, using either zig zag or straight stitch. Each row of stitching must be made in the same direction. The layers of fabric do have a tendency to move and the edges will finish uneven hence the need to cut the panel larger. Work the shorter rows across the long ones. Take care not to allow puckers to form in the corners of the squares. To avoid this you may have to ease the top fabric under the foot. The completed piece of quilting may now be cut to the correct size of the pattern.
Continue to make up the garment in the usual way.
Figure 126 shows two dresses of a very similar pattern but each with its own special design feature.

124

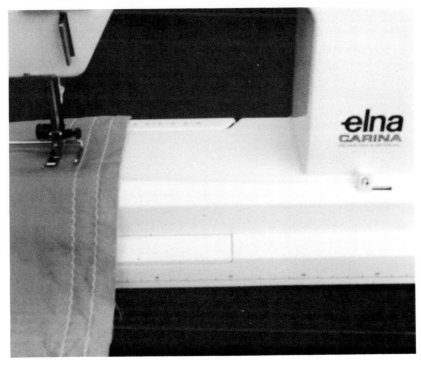

125

Decorative stitches

Decorative stitches may be used to add a personal touch to a garment. Some machines have a built-in selection of stitches while others have drop-in cams or discs. The advantage of drop-in cams is that, as new stitches are developed, they may be added to the existing range but used with the original machine. A vast selection of decorative stitches are available and these may be used for edging, lettering, top stitching etc. Such shapes as rows of ducks, dogs, daisies, stars, hearts, bells etc. may be formed by selecting the appropriate pattern.

An example of the use of a daisy chain is used on the dress in *figure 68*. Here the daisies have been worked between the pin tucking and a very similar pattern has been used as top stitching around the faced neckline.

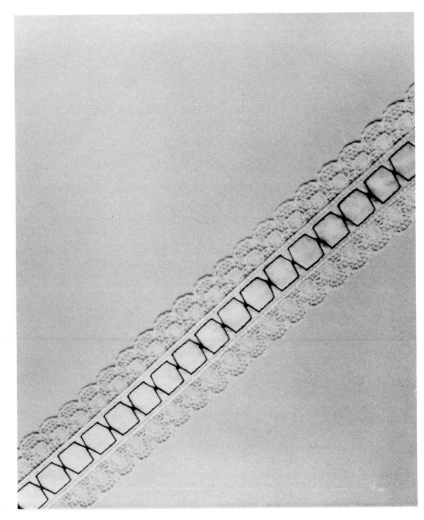

127

I find scallop edging a very useful finish and its use is illustrated in *figure 18*. Here the double yoke has a fold along the lower edge. The yoke has first been edged with scallop edging then laid over the gathered piece and top stitched using the duck pattern. An extremely simple but very pretty finish. The sleeve is scallop edged and elasticated as described in Chapter 3.

A combination of decorative machine stitching and trims such as lace, ribbon, braid or sequins can also be used to good effect. These are particularly useful for nightwear and underwear. *Figure 127* shows a ribbon and lace trim held in place by two rows of blind hem stitches worked opposite each other. This way the simple blind hem stitch forms a most attractive pattern.

Embroidery

Picture embroidery in general is popular for soft furnishing but this does have a limited use in dressmaking. Sports and leisure wear and clothes for young children are the type of garments most likely to lend themselves to embroidery.

The embroidery is carried out by using basic zig zag stitch as a filling stitch. It is necessary to use the darning plate as described in the section on lettering. Some machines require the darning foot where others recommend that no sewing foot is necessary. Either draw a simple picture yourself onto the fabric with a fine pencil or use an embroidery transfer. Stretch the fabric tightly over an embroidery ring. It is best to stitch around the outline of the drawing with straight stitch first to emphasize the lines. Use a matching thread for this purpose. The embroidery may be carried out with a general purpose thread or a special thread intended for embroidery. The general purpose or finer threads seem to give the best results. Work with zig zag stitch set at the widest stitch and with stitch length between 1 and 0. Move and turn the embroidery ring by hand filling in the shapes. Work from the outside towards the centre of each part of the picture as shown in *figure 128*. A great deal of practice may be necessary before you are satisfied with the results and for this reason I would advise you to keep it simple and limit the picture to a patch pocket or small area of the garment.

There are so many ways to incorporate your own personal features into dressmaking. Keep a selection of scraps of fabric. These come in very handy when you wish to add a contrasting fabric for a collar, binding, yoke etc. Mix and match your colours and make full use of the prints available. Checks and stripes lend themselves readily to creating distinctive features as in *figures 17 and 51* where an interesting effect is achieved through cutting certain parts of the garments on the bias of the fabric.

Mixing different textures is another useful way of applying your own personal touch to the garment you are making. An example of this is the pocket in *figure 114*. Be sure that when using fabrics of contrasting texture they are of compatible properties with regard to washing or dry cleaning. Furthermore, make absolutely sure that any braiding, bindings or other trimmings are colour fast and shrink resistant if they are to be used on washable garments.

92

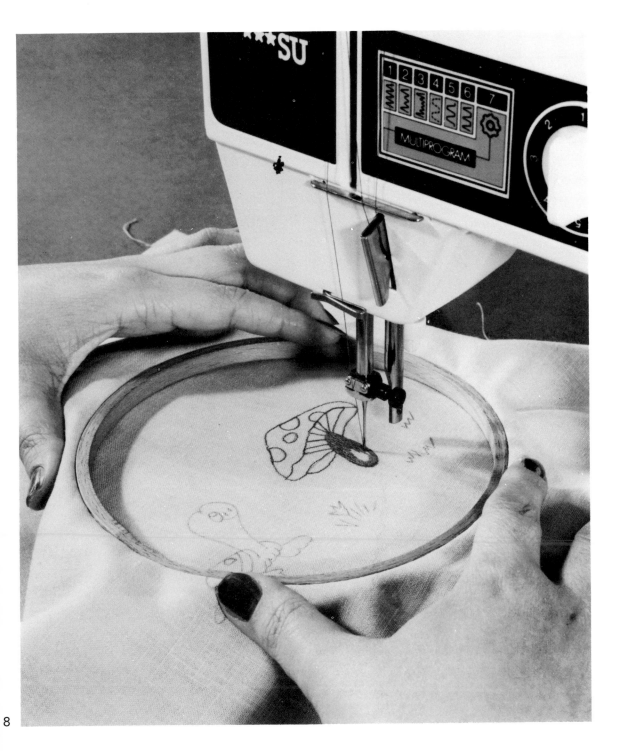

8

List of suppliers

Department stores - dress fabrics and haberdashery

John Lewis Partnership, Oxford Street, London W.1 (and branches)
Harrods, Knightsbridge, London S.W.1
Liberty & Co. Ltd, Regent Street, London W.1
Selfridges, Oxford Street, London W.1

Dress fabrics

Laura Ashley, 71 Lower Sloane Street, London S.W.1 (and branches)
The Fabric Studio, 10 Frith Street, London W.1
H. Wolfin and Son, 64 Great Tichfield Street, London W.1
Strawberry Fayre, Chagford, Newton Abbot, Devon TQ13 8EN
Whaley's (Bradford) Ltd, Ham's Court, Great Horton, Bradford, West Yorkshire BD7 4EQ
Netta (Liskeard) Ltd, 15 & 25 Fore Street, Liskeard, Cornwall
George Weil and Sons Ltd, 63–65 Riding House Street, London W.1

Sewing machines and attachments

Elna Sewing Machines (G.B.) Ltd, 180–182 Tottenham Court Road, London W1P 9LE
Singer Sewing Co. (U.K.) Ltd, 255 High Street, Guildford, Surrey
Bernina Sewing Centre 10 Wardour Street, London W.1
Supreme Sewing Machines, 189 Streatham High Road, London S.W.16

Bedford Sewing and Knitting Machines Ltd, 13 Lime Street, Bedford
Frister & Rossmann Sewing Machines Ltd, Mark Way, Swanley, Kent

Threads and haberdashery

Needle Needs, 20 Beauchamp Place, Knightsbridge, London S.W.1
Tootal Sewing Products, 56 Oxford Street, Manchester M60 1HJ
Perivale-Gutermann Ltd, Wadsworth Road, Perivale, Greenford, Middlesex
McCulloch & Wallis Ltd, 25–26 New Bond Street, London W.1
J. & P. Coats (U.K.) Ltd, Harlequin Avenue, Great West Road, Brentford, Middlesex

Buttons, belts and buckles

Ackerman Buttons Ltd, 326 Hackney Road, London E.2
Button Queen, 19 Marylebone Lane, London W.1
Button Box, 44 Bedford Street, Covent Garden, London W.C.2
Harlequin, Lawling House, Stutton, Ipswich, Suffolk

Sewing aids and interfacings

Value House, 12 Union Road, Croydon, Surrey

The Vilene Organisation, P.O. Box 3, Greetland, Halifax, Yorkshire

¶Index